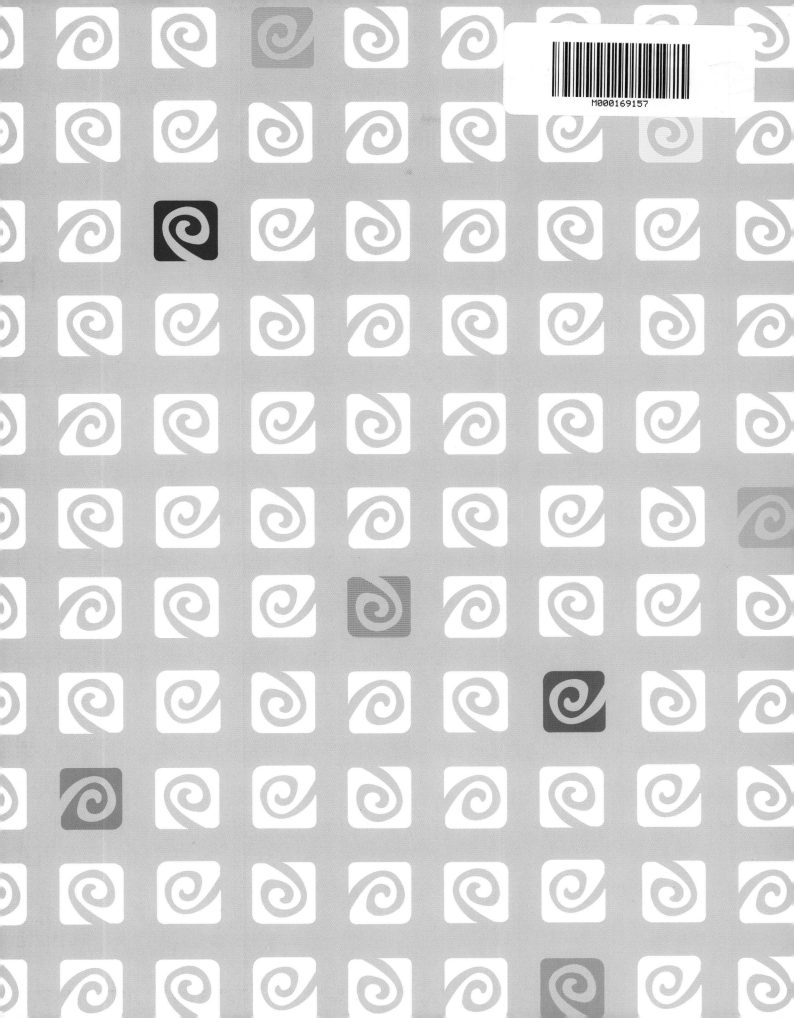

M000169157

TWO-HOUR
PAINTED WOOD PROJECTS

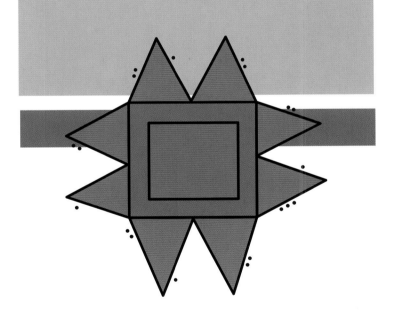

TWO-HOUR
PAINTED WOOD PROJECTS

LINDA DURBANO

Sterling Publishing Co., Inc.   New York
A Sterling / Chapelle Book

CHAPELLE:

Jo Packham, Owner
Cathy Sexton, Editor
Staff:
  Malissa Boatwright
  Rebecca Christensen
  Kellie Cracas
  Holly Hollingsworth
  Susan Jorgensen
  Susan Laws
  Amanda McPeck
  Barbara Milburn
  Leslie Ridenour
  Cindy Rooks
  Cindy Stoeckl
  Nancy Whitley
Kevin Dilley, Photographer
  for Hazen Photography

We wish to thank

for allowing us
to use their
soft sculpture
bunnies
in the photography
for this
publication.

If you have any questions or comments
or would like information on
specialty products featured
in this book, please contact:
Chapelle, Ltd., Inc.
P.O. Box 9252 • Ogden, UT 84409
(801) 621-2777 • (801) 621-2788 Fax

Library of Congress Cataloging-in-Publication Data

Durbano, Linda.
    Two-hour painted wood projects / by Linda Durbano.
        p.   cm.
    "A Sterling / Chapelle book."
    Includes index.
    ISBN 0-8069-1399-1
    1. Painting — Technique. 2. Painted woodwork. 3. Woodwork — Patterns.
    4. Decoration and ornament.   I. Title.
TT385.D87 1996   95-23016
745.7'23 — dc20   CIP

10 9 8 7 6 5 4 3 2 1

Published by Sterling Publishing Company, Inc.
387 Park Avenue South, New York, NY 10016
© 1996 by Chapelle Ltd.
Distributed in Canada by Sterling Publishing
c/o Canadian Manda Group, One Atlantic Avenue, Suite 105
Toronto, Ontario, Canada M6K 3E7
Distributed in Great Britain and Europe by Cassell PLC
Wellington House, 125 Strand, London WC2R 0BB, England
Distributed in Australia by Capricorn Link (Australia) Pty Ltd.
P.O. Box 6651, Baulkham Hills, Business Centre, NSW 2153, Australia
Printed and Bound in Hong Kong
All Rights Reserved

Sterling ISBN 0-8069-1399-1

They say you can pick your friends, but you can't pick your family. I'm fortunate that my family are my friends. Being "Aunt Linda" is one of the greatest joys of my life, and spending time with my family is very precious to me. This book is dedicated to these people I love so deeply.

Much love and thanks to my husband, Dave, for putting up with my "mega-A" personality and for being my very best friend.

Thanks to my editor, Cathy Sexton, for being so good at her job and making mine easier, and thanks to Jo Packham for giving me the opportunity to do this book.

About the Author

Linda Cassity Durbano was born and raised in Ogden, Utah. She has a degree in art and English education from Weber State University.

She owned and operated Piira Prints, Textiles International, originating the "Uncommon Threads" and "Uncommon Borders" fabric series. Linda also designed a line of fabrics called the "Brass Ring Collection" for Springs Industries, New York.

Before becoming marketing vice president for The Western Group, an association of shortline railroads, she owned a newsletter business for three years. Linda now directs all marketing activities for the Verde Canyon Railroad in Clarkdale, Arizona, and the Wyoming Scenic Railroad in Laramie, Wyoming.

Linda is married to David L. Durbano, has six stepchildren, and five grandchildren. She now resides in Laramie, Wyoming, but still maintains a residence in Ogden, Utah.

Table of Contents

General Instructions

When creating pieces for this book, every attempt was made to make them legitimate 2-hour projects. This time period excludes shopping for materials and any time spent in preparing woods for painting. I hope you enjoy painting these projects, as much as I enjoyed creating them!

Before You Begin:

Many of the projects in this book call for wood shapes that we have provided dimensions and patterns for use in cutting these shapes. However, anytime you are able to find pre-cut pieces, we recommend you do just that! We want you to get on with the "painting" of these projects—that's why this book was written!

Transferring Patterns:

If you cannot find pre-cut wood shapes you need for a particular project, you will need to cut them from wood using the dimensions and patterns provided for your use. When doing so, you will trace the patterns from this book onto tracing paper using a pencil. You will use graphite paper to transfer these patterns onto the wood shapes. Be certain that you take all precautions in cutting the wood shapes from the wood—safety always comes first!

After you have cut the wood shapes that you need, lightly sand all edges and rough surfaces with fine- or medium-grit sandpaper. Using a clean, damp cloth, wipe the dust from the sanded shapes.

Spackling / Texturing Techniques:

Using a spackling knife or a metal ruler, apply spackling compound to the surface and texture as desired. Be sure to use a spackling compound that can be painted. Let the spackling compound dry completely before painting. A texturing medium can also be used by following manufacturer's instructions.

Dry Brushing:

You will use a 1/2" flat brush to dry brush—make sure the flat brush is indeed dry. Dip the dry, flat brush into the acrylic paint and brush across a piece of paper until most of the paint is removed from the bristles of the brush. Paint the surface. Repeat this process as necessary for coverage desired.

Stenciling:

You can either use a pre-cut stencil or cut one yourself by tracing the pattern onto poster board or a manila envelope and cutting it out carefully with a craft knife or scissors. Using your fingertips, hold the stencil firmly in place on your project.

To get the best results, use a stencil brush as they are designed so that paint can be applied vertically without seeping under the edges. Apply acrylic paint with a gentle, dabbing motion, working well into the edges for a clean line. Don't overload the brush with acrylic paint, but instead "dab" several coats for a more intense color.

Painting with a Toothbrush:

Dip an old toothbrush into the stain or acrylic paint you intend to use. Using your finger, "flip" the mixture onto the project from a distance of about six inches. Let the stain or acrylic paint dry.

Rag Painting Techniques:

Using a clean, dry textured rag or cheesecloth, dip the corner of the rag into acrylic paint and blot the excess paint onto a paper towel. Dab the rag over the surface to be painted, using heavy or light coverage as desired.

Antiquing:

Using an old pie pan, pour a small amount of mineral spirits or paint thinner in one side and a small amount of acrylic paint in the other side. Thin your paint a little at a time.

Using an old brush or a disposable sponge brush, apply this stain over the surface. Let the stain dry for about 30 seconds and, using a rag or old cloth, wipe off the remaining stain.

When covering a large area, do a small portion at a time, overlapping so as to not leave an unwanted pattern. If the stain is too dark, some may be removed with a rag dipped in mineral spirits or paint thinner and if a darker stain is desired, simply repeat the process.

All rags and brushes should be disposed of properly, as the stain mixture makes these items very combustible.

Sponge Painting:

Using a small damp sponge, dip into acrylic paint and "blot" onto paper towels to remove excess paint before "blotting" the surface of the project, using heavy or light coverage as desired.

An Angel Stood Guard
at the Golden Gate

I used this angel twice in the book. I created a very serious piece with her, but knew she had extended value when creating this birdhouse. The idea was outrageous, so I tried to keep the project simple in color and shape. I think it is a piece that every birdhouse collector needs to add to his or her collection. It will join my mother's collection.

THINGS YOU'LL NEED:

Birdhouse,
   9" tall x 4" wide x 4" deep,
   with a steeple
Angel,
   6" x 14" x $1/8$" balsa wood
Wings,
   6" x 10" x $1/8$" balsa wood
5 Wooden star buttons
$1^3/4$" Wooden star
Pencil
Tracing paper
Graphite paper
$1/2$" Flat brush
Small pointed brush
1" Sponge brush
Carving knife or
   heavy-duty X-acto knife
Fine-grit sandpaper
Clean cloth

White primer
Acrylic paint:
   Metallic gold
   Pale pink
   Royal blue
   Sedona clay
   Wicker white
Oil paint:
   Burnt umber
Mineral spirits
Rag or old cloth
Fine-point permanent
   gold marker
Fine-point permanent
   black marker
Glue gun and glue sticks
Clear matte spray finish
White thread and needle

FOLLOW THESE STEPS:

For the Angel:

1 Cut the angel and the wings from the $1/8$" balsa wood. Use the patterns from page 13. Refer to the General Instructions for transferring patterns.

2 Using a carving knife or a heavy-duty X-acto knife, remove small pieces of wood from the edges of the angel, the wings, and the $1^3/4$" wooden star so they appear to have been hand-carved.

3 Using a pencil, trace the pattern on the front and back of the angel's body onto tracing paper. Using graphite paper, transfer the pattern onto the wood. Refer to the pattern.

11

4 Using a 1/2" flat brush, paint the angel's dress and shoes with wicker white acrylic paint. Paint the wings with metallic gold acrylic paint. Paint the wooden star buttons and the 1 3/4" wooden star with metallic gold acrylic paint. Using the small pointed brush, paint the angel's legs, hands, and face with pale pink acrylic paint. When painting, leave the pencil or traced line unpainted so the wood is exposed. When the figure is stained, the stain will remain in the unpainted areas and create an outline. Paint the back side of the angel. Use the same pattern to paint the legs, hands, and shoes as used on the front of the angel. Let the paint dry between coats.

5 Paint the hair on the front and the back side of the angel with Sedona clay acrylic paint, leaving pencil lines exposed. Mix Sedona clay and pale pink acrylic paints and paint irregular circles on the angel's cheeks. Let the paint dry between coats.

6 Using the needle and white thread, sew through the holes in the star buttons. Loop through the button holes with double strands of thread about three times.

7 Mix 1 part of burnt umber oil paint to 5 parts of mineral spirits. Using a 1" sponge brush, paint this stain over the front of the angel. Let the stain dry for about 20 seconds and, using a rag or old cloth, wipe off the remaining stain. Repeat this process on the back side of the angel, the 1 3/4" star, and the wings.

8 Using a fine-point permanent black marker, dot the eyes onto the face and draw a small arc for the angel's smile. Refer to the pattern. Draw a 5" line from the chin of the angel down the center of her dress. Draw a collar and place small dots around the bottom edge of the collar. Draw a line across the hem of the dress about 3/8" from the bottom. Add small dots between the line and bottom hem of the dress. Draw a line about 1/8" from where the sleeve meets the hand. Repeat the sleeve and hem design on the back of the dress.

9 Using a glue gun, attach the star buttons on top of the line drawn down the center of the dress. Refer to the pattern for suggested placement. Attach one point of the wooden star halo to the top of her head. Attach the wings to the back of the angel so the arch of the wings appears to be coming from the bottom of her hairline. Using clear matte spray finish, spray both sides of the angel and the wings. Apply additional coats of spray finish to the angel and wings. Let the spray finish dry between coats.

For the Birdhouse:

1 Using fine-grit sandpaper, lightly sand the birdhouse. Using a clean, damp cloth, wipe the dust from the birdhouse.

2 Using the 1" sponge brush, paint the birdhouse with white primer. Let the primer dry. Using the 1/2" flat brush, paint the birdhouse with royal blue acrylic paint. Leave brush strokes and overlapping paint strokes. Some of the white primer may show through the royal blue acrylic paint. Using the 1/2" flat brush, dry-brush white clouds over the royal blue acrylic paint with wicker white acrylic paint. Refer to the photograph for suggested placement. Let the paint dry between coats. Refer to the General Instructions for dry brushing.

3 Using the pencil, trace the lettering pattern from page 13 onto tracing paper. Using graphite paper, transfer the lettering to the birdhouse above the opening. Using the fine-point permanent gold marker, trace the lettering.

4 Using clear matte spray finish, spray the birdhouse. Apply additional coats of spray finish to the birdhouse. Let the spray finish dry between coats.

5 Using the glue gun, attach the angel to the birdhouse by gluing the back of the angel's legs to the steeple of the birdhouse. The angel's feet should appear as though she is standing on the roof of the birdhouse.

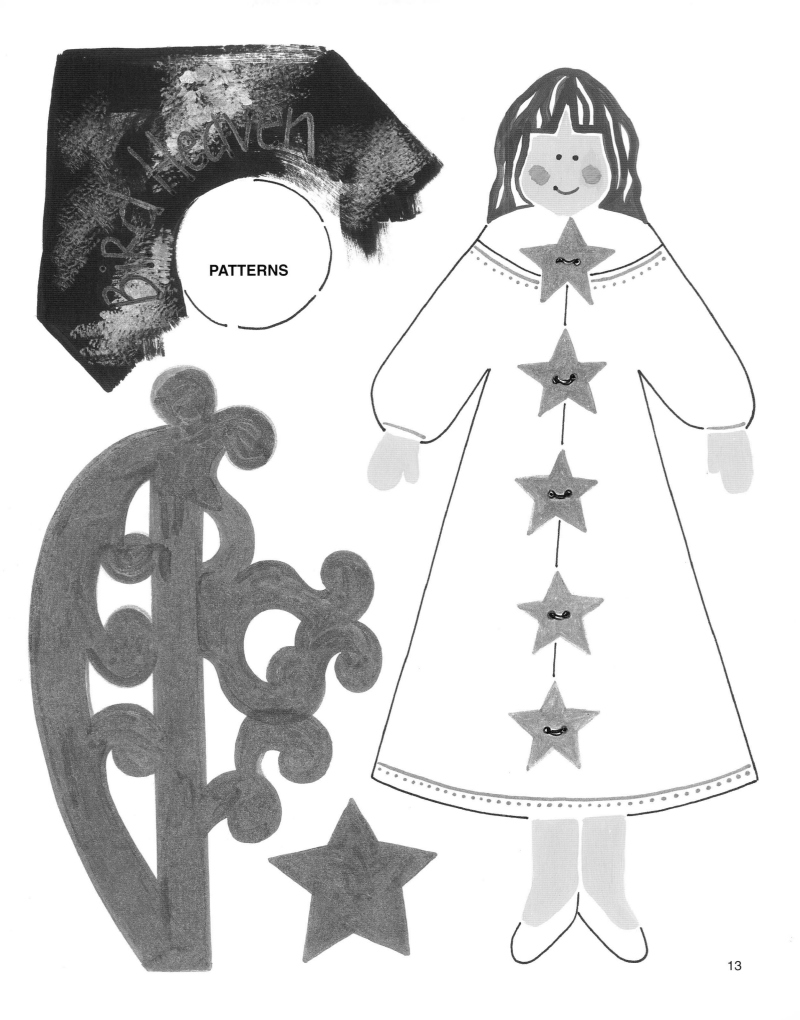

PATTERNS

13

A Plate Full of Cherries

This is one of my favorite projects in this book. The simplicity of the design is what appeals to me. Also, the simple coloring will work well in any room of my home. I think the plate would look good on the mantel in my living room, on the antique dresser in my entry, or on the buffet in my dining room. It is nice to have choices in life!

THINGS YOU'LL NEED:

15$\frac{1}{2}$" Wooden plate
  with a 3" rim
Ruler
Pencil
Eraser
Tracing paper
Graphite paper
$\frac{1}{2}$" Flat brush
1" Sponge brush
Acrylic paint:
  Barnyard red
  Butter pecan
  Linen beige
  Thicket green
Oil paint:
  Burnt umber
Mineral spirits
Rag or old cloth
Fine-point permanent
  black marker
Clear matte spray finish

FOLLOW THESE STEPS:

1 Using a ruler, divide the center of the wooden plate into 1" squares by drawing lines with a pencil.

2 Using the pencil, trace the cherry pattern from page 16 onto tracing paper. Using graphite paper, transfer the pattern onto the plate rim. Refer to the photograph for suggested placement. For variety, you may opt to reverse the pattern for some of the cherries. Draw a leaf next to

the cherries, and vice versa, so that not too many cherries or leaves are together.

3 Using a $\frac{1}{2}$" flat brush, working in the circular direction of the plate rim, paint the plate rim with butter pecan acrylic paint. Apply only one thin coat of paint to allow the wood to be exposed through the paint. Let the paint dry.

4 Paint the squares in the center of the plate, alternating squares with butter pecan acrylic paint and linen beige acrylic paint. Leave a small amount of space around each square, near the pencil markings, unpainted. Refer to Diagram A. Let the paint dry between coats.

5 Paint inside the plate rim, between the center of the plate and the outside rim, with linen beige acrylic paint. Let the paint dry. The back of the plate will not be painted with acrylic paint.

6 Paint the cherries with barnyard red acrylic paint. Paint the leaves and stems with thicket green acrylic paint. Let the paint dry.

7 Mix 1 part of burnt umber oil paint to 4 parts of mineral spirits. Using a 1" sponge brush, paint this stain over the entire plate front and sides. Let the stain dry for about 30 seconds and, using a rag or old cloth, wipe off the remaining stain. Using the stain, repeat the process on the back of the plate.

8 Using an eraser, erase all the exposed pencil lines on the front of the plate. Using a fine-point permanent black marker, draw small circles on the plate rim around the cherries and at the corners of every other square on the center of the plate. Refer to the photograph for suggested placement. Outline and add small dots to the cherries, the stems, and the leaves. Draw a line down the center of each leaf. Dots and lines may vary from cherry to cherry and leaf to leaf. Refer to the photograph for suggested placement.

9 Using clear matte spray finish, spray the front of the plate. Let the spray finish dry. Using the spray finish, repeat the process on the back of the plate. Let the spray finish dry. Apply additional coats of spray finish to the front of the plate if the plate will be used to serve food.

PATTERN

DIAGRAM A

Idea: Lemon or acorn patterns for your plate rim

Get
Those
Coats
Out

Get Those Coats Out

This coat rack was purchased by my sister, Nan, with instructions to me to make her something that could hang above her bathroom window with raffia draped from the pegs for a window treatment. As I write this, she hasn't seen it. I am hoping she and her husband, Allen, will approve. If not, I have a few vacant windows.

THINGS YOU'LL NEED:

Coat rack, 30" x 3$\frac{1}{2}$" x $\frac{3}{4}$", with five 3" wooden pegs
4 Trees, 5" x 10" x $\frac{1}{8}$" balsa wood
$\frac{3}{4}$" Masking tape
$\frac{1}{2}$" Flat brush
1" Sponge brush
Spackling knife or metal ruler
Spackling compound
Fine-grit sandpaper
Clean cloth
Acrylic paint:
   Acorn brown
   Butter pecan
   Dark green
   Mint green
Oil paint:
   Burnt umber
Mineral spirits
Rag or old cloth
Glue gun and glue sticks
Clear matte spray finish

FOLLOW THESE STEPS:

1 Cut the trees from the $\frac{1}{8}$" balsa wood. Use the tree pattern from page 19. Refer to the General Instructions for transferring patterns. Using $\frac{3}{4}$" masking tape, tape around all the front edges of the coat rack. Be sure the masking tape is pushed down securely on the wood so that paint cannot seep under the edges of the tape.

2 Using either a spackling knife or a metal ruler, spackle inside the masking tape lines and around the

wooden pegs with spackling compound. Texture the trees with spackling compound. Refer to the General Instructions for spackling and texturing techniques. Let the spackling compound dry completely.

3 Using fine-grit sandpaper, lightly sand all spackled and textured surfaces. Using a clean, damp cloth, wipe the dust from the coat rack and the trees.

4 Using a $\frac{1}{2}$" flat brush, paint some areas of the trees and all of the tree edges with dark green acrylic paint. Paint the remaining areas of the trees with mint green acrylic paint. Refer to the pattern. Repeat the process on the coat rack with acorn brown and butter pecan acrylic paints. Let the paint dry between coats.

5 Dry-brush the trees and coat rack with butter pecan acrylic paint. Refer to the General Instructions for dry brushing techniques.

6 Paint the wooden pegs with acorn brown acrylic paint. Let the paint dry.

7 Mix 1 part of burnt umber oil paint to 3 parts of mineral spirits. Using a 1" sponge brush, paint this stain over the painted coat rack. Let the stain dry for about 30 seconds and, using a rag or old cloth, wipe off the remaining stain. Using the stain, repeat the process on the wooden pegs and the trees.

8 Using a glue gun, attach the trees to the coat rack between the wooden pegs. Two of the trees are attached over the holes where the nails or screws go to hang the coat rack. If you are hanging the coat rack in this manner, you may want to hang it, and then attach the trees.

9 Remove the masking tape. Using clear matte spray finish, spray the coat rack and the trees. Apply a second coat of spray finish to the coat rack and trees. Let the spray finish dry between coats.

PATTERN

Idea: Instead of trees how about a planter or a teddy bear for the baby's room!

19

Hop to It

Our Wyoming Scenic Railroad excursion manager, Mollie Smith, just had her first child. We had a shower for Mollie and her husband, Kenny, at our ranch house. It was during calving season and everyone at the shower went to the barn to observe the birth of a calf. Can you believe we did that to her? I just couldn't bring myself to put a cow on this frame.

THINGS YOU'LL NEED:

Wooden frame,
  9$^{1}/_{2}$" x 9$^{1}/_{2}$" x $^{3}/_{4}$" pine
  with 4$^{1}/_{2}$" square opening
Rabbit, 11" x 6" x $^{3}/_{4}$" pine
2 Carrots,
  6$^{1}/_{2}$" x 2" x $^{3}/_{4}$" pine
Star stencil with
  2" and $^{7}/_{8}$" star cutouts
$^{1}/_{2}$"-Square stencil
$^{1}/_{2}$" Flat brush
Stencil brush
1" Sponge brush
Spackling knife or metal ruler
Spackling compound
Fine-grit sandpaper
Clean cloth
Acrylic paint:
  Avocado green
  Butter pecan
  Mint green
  Sedona clay
  White

Oil paint:
  Burnt umber
Mineral spirits
Rag or old cloth
Glue gun and glue sticks
  or Tacky glue
Clear matte spray finish

FOLLOW THESE STEPS:

1 Cut the rabbit and the carrots from the $^{3}/_{4}$" pine. Use the patterns from page 22. Refer to the General Instructions for transferring patterns.

2 Using either a spackling knife or a metal ruler, spackle one side and all of the edges of the frame, the rabbit, and the carrots with spackling compound. Refer to the General Instructions for spackling and texturing techniques. Let the spackling compound dry completely.

3 Using fine-grit sandpaper, lightly sand all spackled and textured surfaces. Using a clean, damp cloth, wipe the dust from the frame, the rabbit, and the carrots.

4 Using a ¹/₂" flat brush, paint the front and the sides of the rabbit with butter pecan acrylic paint. Paint the carrots with Sedona clay acrylic paint and paint the carrot tops with avocado green acrylic paint. Paint the frame with mint green acrylic paint. Let the paint dry.

5 Using the ¹/₂"-square stencil and the stencil brush, stencil squares onto the frame with white acrylic paint. Refer to the photograph. The squares are *not* evenly distributed around the opening of the frame. Using

the 2" star stencil and white acrylic paint, stencil large stars onto the rabbit. Using the ⁷/₈" star stencil and white acrylic paint, stencil small stars onto the carrots. Let the paint dry.

6 Mix 1 part of burnt umber oil paint to 4 parts of mineral spirits. Using a 1" sponge brush, paint this stain over the front and sides of the painted frame. Let the stain dry for about 30 seconds and, using a rag or old cloth, wipe off the remaining stain. Using the stain, repeat the process on the rabbit and the carrots.

If the stain is too dark, clean the surfaces with clear mineral spirits and repeat the process using less burnt umber oil paint.

7 Using a glue gun or Tacky glue, attach the rabbit and the carrots. Refer to the photograph for suggested placement.

8 Using clear matte spray finish, spray the front and sides of the frame, the rabbit, and the carrots. Apply a second coat of spray finish to the frame, rabbit, and carrots. Let the spray finish dry between coats.

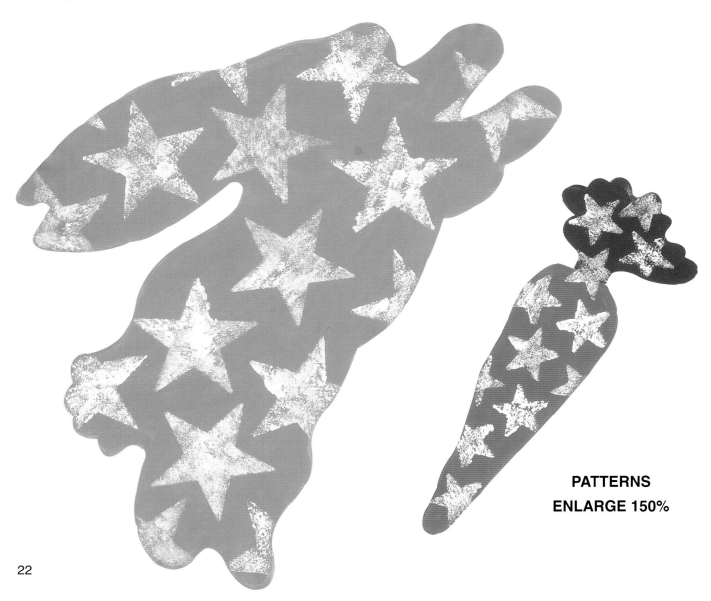

**PATTERNS
ENLARGE 150%**

Idea:
cowboy boot
& hat for
the frame...

...or a
series of hearts

23

Laramie Cow

Cows, cows, and more cows! I have learned more about cows over the past year than I thought there was to know. Our ranch hands, Derek, Penni, and John, know more about cows and horses than I'll know in a lifetime. They're good teachers, but I'd better stick to golf and snow skiing.

THINGS YOU'LL NEED:

12" x 12" x ⁵/₈" pine or
  6" x 24" x ⁵/₈" pine
Pencil
¹/₂" Flat brush
1" Sponge brush
Carving knife or
  heavy-duty X-acto knife
Fine-grit sandpaper
Clean cloth
Acrylic paint:
  Chocolate brown
  Linen beige
Oil paint:
  Burnt umber
Mineral spirits
Rag or old cloth
Tacky glue or wood glue
Clear matte spray finish

FOLLOW THESE STEPS:

1 Cut the cow pieces from the ⁵/₈" pine. Cut out one body, two legs, and one set of horns. Use the cow patterns from page 27. Refer to the General Instructions for transferring patterns.

2 Using fine-grit sandpaper, lightly sand all wood surfaces. Using a clean, damp cloth, wipe the dust from the wood shapes.

3 Using a carving knife or a heavy-duty X-acto knife, remove small pieces of wood from the edges of the wood shapes so they appear to have been hand-carved. Do not carve edges where the legs and the body meet.

4 Place the pieces of the wood together to make sure all pieces fit together correctly before gluing. Refer to the photograph for placement. Remove the pieces and apply Tacky glue or wood glue. Place the pieces together and let the glue dry.

5 Using a 1" sponge brush, paint the entire cow with linen beige acrylic paint. Let the paint dry.

6 Using a pencil, draw irregular circles and ovals on the cow's body, face, and legs. Refer to the pattern for suggested placement. Using a 1/2" flat brush, paint the irregular circles and ovals with chocolate brown acrylic paint. Let the paint dry.

7 Mix 1 part of burnt umber oil paint to 4 parts of mineral spirits. Using the sponge brush, paint this stain over one side of the cow. Let the stain dry for about 30 seconds and, using a rag or old cloth, wipe off the remaining stain. Using the stain, repeat the process on the other side of the cow and all remaining wood shapes.

8 Using the sponge brush, apply a small amount of undiluted burnt umber oil paint to the edges of the cow in the grooved knife marks. Let the stain dry.

9 Using clear matte spray finish, spray the cow. Apply a second coat of spray finish to the cow. Let the spray finish dry between coats.

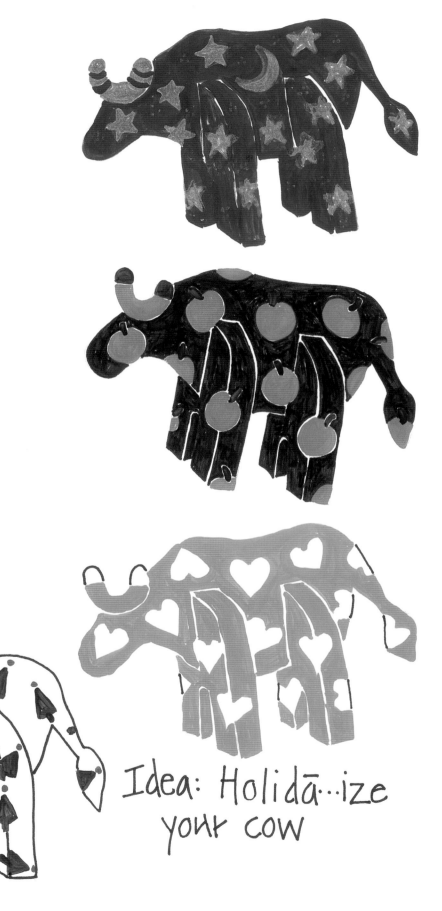

Idea: Holidā...ize your cow

26

PATTERNS

Picture Perfect

I love stars. Our Wyoming ranch is 22 miles from the closest town. Without the interruption of earthly light, the stars are abundant and beautiful. Their brilliance makes me ponder all of life's mysteries ... and wonder why I'm up so late when I have to get up early to feed the orphaned calves. Who knows what this has to do with this frame!

THINGS YOU'LL NEED:

6 Wooden balls,
  $1/2$" diameter
Wooden frame,
  $4^1/_2$" x $5^1/_2$"
  with $1^3/_4$" x $2^3/_4$" opening
1" Sponge brush
$1/2$" Flat brush
Fine-grit sandpaper
Clean cloth
Acrylic paint:
  Black
  Navy
Medium-point permanent
  gold marker
Glue gun and glue sticks
Clear matte spray finish

DIAGRAM A

FOLLOW THESE STEPS:

1 Remove the backing and the glass from the frame.

2 Using fine-grit sandpaper, lightly sand the frame. Using a clean, damp cloth, wipe the dust from the frame.

3 Using a $1/2$" flat brush, paint the inside edges by the frame opening with black acrylic paint. Using a 1" sponge brush, paint the front and outside edges of the frame with navy acrylic paint. Let the paint dry.

4 Using a medium-point permanent gold marker, color the six wooden balls. Let the marker dry.

5 Using the medium-point permanent gold marker, make spirals and stars on the frame. Use small dots to create the image. Refer to Diagram A.

6 Using a glue gun, attach the wooden balls to the top of the frame. Refer to the photograph for placement.

7 Using clear matte spray finish, spray the frame and the wooden balls. Apply a second coat of spray finish to the frame and wooden balls. Let the spray finish dry between coats.

8 Return the glass to the frame. Insert your favorite photograph and return the backing to the frame.

Blocks Cubed

I don't want to mislead you in thinking that these three blocks can be created in two hours. You can actually "paint" one block in two hours, but setting up the designs will take longer. These blocks are going to end up in my friend Jo's house. They were created with her in mind, and when she saw them she said, "I want these for Christmas!"

THINGS YOU'LL NEED:

3 Wooden blocks,
   4" square
Pencil
Tracing paper
Graphite paper
Small pointed brush
Acrylic paint:
   Beige
   Burnt orange
   Charcoal black
   Dark green
Pale green
Pink
Purple
Red
Royal blue
White
Yellow
Fine-point permanent
   gold marker
Medium-point permanent
   gold marker
Clear matte spray finish

FOLLOW THESE STEPS:

1 Using a pencil, trace one pattern from page 32 onto tracing paper. Using graphite paper, transfer the pattern onto one side of one wooden block. Repeat the process for the remaining patterns on pages 33 and 34. Three patterns will need to be repeated to complete a set of six designs per block—you choose your favorites!

2 Using a small pointed brush, paint the wooden blocks with acrylic paint. Start with the light-colored acrylic paints, finishing with the darkest-colored acrylic paints. It is easiest to paint all three wooden blocks at the same time. This allows the paint to dry before turning the blocks over to paint the other sides

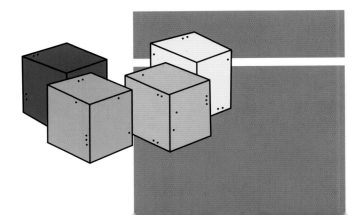

with the same colors. Don't worry about the fine, detailed edges because you will outline them using a fine-point permanent gold marker. Refer to the patterns here and on pages 33 and 34 for suggested colors for painting.

3 Using a medium-point permanent gold marker, paint all of the edges of the wooden blocks between the designs. Again, it is easiest to paint all three wooden blocks at the same time, allowing the paint to dry before turning the blocks over to paint the other sides with the marker.

4 Using the fine-point permanent gold marker, outline the figures which are to be outlined with gold. Refer to the patterns.

5 Using clear matte spray finish, spray all sides of each wooden block. Let the spray finish dry before turning the blocks over. Be careful not to get too close to the blocks while you are applying the spray finish, as it could cause the markers to run. Apply a second coat of spray finish to the blocks. Let the spray finish dry.

PATTERNS

Hitchin'
a Ride

Hitchin' a Ride

I love rabbits and different rabbit shapes. This shape was actually one I developed for a flyer I created years ago. I recycled it from my portfolio and thought it would work with this little wagon. The entire piece is very simple, which fits my taste, especially when adding nature's best — foliage and flowers!

THINGS YOU'LL NEED:

Wooden wagon
4 Rabbits,
    12" x 12" x $\frac{1}{8}$" balsa wood
4 Wooden hearts,
    3" x 12" x $\frac{1}{8}$" balsa wood
$\frac{1}{2}$" Flat brush
Small pointed brush
Carving knife or
    heavy-duty X-acto knife
Fine-grit sandpaper
Clean cloth
Acrylic paint:
    Butter pecan
    Sedona clay
    Dark green
Glue gun and glue sticks
Clear matte spray finish

FOLLOW THESE STEPS:

1 Cut the rabbits and the hearts from the balsa wood. Use the rabbit and heart patterns from page 37. Refer to the General Instructions for transferring patterns.

2 Using a carving knife or a heavy-duty X-acto knife, remove small pieces of wood from the edges of the wood rabbits and hearts so they appear to have been hand-carved. Carve only one edge of the wooden hearts.

3 Using a $\frac{1}{2}$" flat brush, paint the front and the sides of the rabbits with butter pecan acrylic paint. Paint the back of the rabbits with butter pecan acrylic paint. Paint the front and the sides of the hearts with Sedona clay acrylic paint. Let the paint dry between coats.

4 Paint the inside and the outside of the wagon with dark green acrylic paint. Paint the wagon wheels with butter pecan acrylic paint. Paint the wagon dowels and undercarriage with Sedona clay acrylic paint. Let the paint dry.

5 Using fine-grit sandpaper, lightly sand the edges of the rabbits, the hearts, the wagon, the dowels, the wheels, and the undercarriage. Using a clean, damp cloth, wipe the dust from the sanded pieces.

6 Using a glue gun, attach the hearts to the center of one side of each rabbit. Attach the rabbits to the sides of the wagon. Refer to the photograph for suggested placement.

7 Using a small pointed brush, paint small dots around the outside rim of each wagon wheel with Sedona clay acrylic paint. Let the paint dry.

8 Using clear matte spray finish, spray the wagon and the rabbits. Apply a second coat of spray finish to the wagon and rabbits. Let the spray finish dry between coats.

**PATTERNS
ENLARGE 115%**

Idea:
Replace your
bunny with a
lamb or a white
picket fence

Planted Pots

My brother, Mike, and his wife, Linda, have the green thumbs in my family. These little pots will look good in their tidy new kitchen greenhouse window. And, chances are, the plants will live!

THINGS YOU'LL NEED:

3 Clay pots,
   3¹/₂" diameter
Pencil
Tracing paper
Graphite paper
1" Sponge brush
Small pointed brush
Acrylic paint:
   Butter pecan
   Sedona clay
   Dark green
Clear matte spray finish

FOLLOW THESE STEPS:

1 Using a 1" sponge brush, paint the body of two clay pots and the top rim of the third clay pot with dark green acrylic paint. Apply as many coats as necessary to cover. Let the paint dry between each coat.

2 Using a small pointed brush, paint three horizontal stripes around the rim of one of the clay pots that has an unpainted top rim. Allow the brush stroke to become thinner and thicker as you paint.

3 Using a pencil, trace the heart pattern below onto tracing paper. Using graphite paper, transfer the pattern onto the rims of the two remaining clay pots. Eleven hearts should be transferred onto each clay pot.

4 Using the small pointed brush, paint the hearts on the clay pot that has been painted dark green with butter pecan acrylic paint. Paint the hearts on the clay pot that has the top rim painted dark green with Sedona clay acrylic paint.

PATTERN

5 Using the small pointed brush, paint small dots with dark green acrylic paint between the butter pecan colored hearts—approximately five dots. Paint small dots with butter pecan acrylic paint between the Sedona clay colored hearts. Paint dots around the top and the bottom of the rim that has the horizontal lines with butter pecan acrylic paint. Refer to the photograph for suggested placement.

6 Using clear matte spray finish, spray the clay pots. Apply a second coat of spray finish to the clay pots. Let the spray finish dry between coats. Plant your favorite flowers.

Idea: change the coloring & patterns on the rims of the pots. Paint planters to match. Don't be afraid to experiment with color!

Mama Kitty on My Mind

I have a 13-year-old black cat named Mama Kitty. She is stuck-up and demanding, but I love her. She adopted all of our dogs and keeps their faces spit-shined. She can create some fantastic doggie-dos with cat saliva. When the alarm rings, it will remind me of Mama Kitty, long after she is gone.

THINGS YOU'LL NEED:

Wooden clock,
 4 1/4" square x 2" deep
4 Finials, 1" x 4"
3 Cats,
 2" x 4" x 3/4" pine
3/4" Masking tape
1/2" Flat brush
Fine-grit sandpaper
Clean cloth
Acrylic paint:
 Black
 Mustard, optional
Glue gun and glue sticks
Clear matte spray finish

FOLLOW THESE STEPS:

1 Cut the cats from the 3/4" pine. Use the cat pattern below. Refer to the General Instructions for transferring patterns.

2 Using fine-grit sandpaper, lightly sand the clock and the cats. Using a clean, damp cloth, wipe the dust from the clock and the cats.

3 Using 3/4" masking tape, cover the clock mechanism.

4 Using a 1/2" flat brush, paint the finials and the cats with black acrylic paint.

5 Using the 1/2" flat brush, paint the clock the color of your choice — I chose mustard acrylic paint. Apply as many coats as necessary to cover. Let the paint dry between coats.

6 Using a glue gun, attach one finial to each corner on the bottom of the clock. Attach the cats to the top of the clock. Refer to the photograph for suggested placement. Two cats should be facing one direction and the other cat should be facing the opposite direction.

7 Using clear matte spray finish, spray the clock. Let the spray finish dry. Remove the masking tape from the clock mechanism, insert the batteries, and set the time!

PATTERN

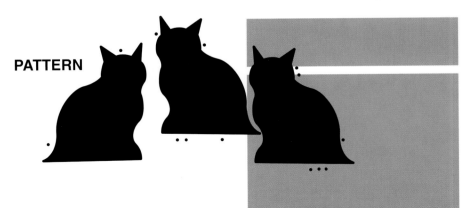

Such Chair-acter!

I think miniature chairs are a kick! I've always liked tiny things and these small chairs are no exception. Although they are attractive on their own, I thought it would be fun to decorate them and add a few accessory pieces. The pieces can be removed or added with your mood or the season.

THINGS YOU'LL NEED:

For the Quilted Tree Chair:

Miniature grapevine chair,
  11" tall with a
  4½" x 4½" seat
Wooden tree,
  5" x 5" x ¼" pine
Wooden heart,
  2" x 2" x ⅛" balsa wood
Raw canvas,
  4¼" x 4¼"
Quilting stencil
  with at least four
  1¾" designs
Pencil
¼" Flat brush
Small pointed brush
Fine-grit sandpaper
Clean cloth
Acrylic paint:
  Barnyard red
  Dark green
Glue gun and glue sticks
Clear matte spray finish
Cotton batting, 4¼" x 4¼"
Cotton fabric, 4¼" x 4¼"

FOLLOW THESE STEPS:

1 Cut the tree from the ¼" pine and the heart from the ⅛" balsa wood. Use the patterns from page 44. Refer to the General Instructions for transferring patterns.

2 Using a ¼" flat brush, paint one side and all the edges of the tree with dark green acrylic paint. Paint one side and all the edges of the heart with barnyard red acrylic paint. Let the paint dry between coats.

3 Using fine-grit sandpaper, lightly sand the edges of the heart. Sand the edges of the tree, taking more paint off the corners of the pointed limbs. Using a clean, damp cloth, wipe the dust from the heart and the tree.

4 Using a glue gun, attach the heart to the center of the tree. Refer to the photograph for suggested placement.

5 Using a pencil, draw a ⅜" border around the perimeter of the raw canvas. Refer to the pattern. Inside, draw four 1¾" squares. Continue these lines to the outside perimeter of the canvas. Using the quilting stencil, draw the four different designs in each of the 1¾" squares.

6 Using a small pointed brush, paint these areas with barnyard red and dark green acrylic paints. Refer to the pattern. Let the paint dry. Leave a small amount of space around each color unpainted. Apply only one thin coat of paint to allow the canvas to be exposed through the paint. This will make the seat cover look more rustic.

7 Using clear matte spray finish, spray the canvas. Spray the tree and let the spray finish dry. Apply a second coat of spray finish to the tree. Let the spray finish dry.

8 Place the cotton batting between the wrong side of the canvas and the wrong side of the cotton fabric. Sew the fabric and the canvas together using a 1/8" seam allowance.

9 Using the glue gun, attach the tree to the back of the chair. Refer to the photograph for suggested placement. If preferred, permanently attach the cushion to the chair's seat.

PATTERNS

44

THINGS YOU'LL NEED:

For the Southwest Chair:

Miniature grapevine chair,
  8¹/₂" tall with a
  4" x 4" seat
Cowboy hat,
  4" x 6" x ¹/₈" balsa wood
Star,
  1" x 1" x ¹/₈" balsa wood
2 Snakes,
  4" x 5" x ¹/₈" balsa wood
2 Silver feathers
Pencil
¹/₂" Flat brush
Small pointed brush
Fine-grit sandpaper
Clean cloth
Acrylic paint:
  Lavender
  Moon yellow
  Red brick
  Turquoise
Glue gun and glue sticks
Clear matte spray finish

FOLLOW THESE STEPS:

1 Cut the cowboy hat, the star, and the snakes from the ¹/₈" balsa wood. Use the patterns from pages 44 and 45. Refer to the General Instructions for transferring patterns.

2 Using a pencil, sketch the designs on the cowboy hat and the snakes. Refer to the patterns. Because you will be using such small quantities of acrylic paint, it is easier to paint all three pieces at once.

3 Using a ¹/₂" flat brush or a small pointed brush, paint the cowboy hat and the snakes. Refer to the patterns for suggested colors for painting. Before painting, make sure the snakes face each other. Refer to the photograph. Paint the star with moon yellow acrylic paint. Let the paint dry between coats.

4 Using fine-grit sandpaper, lightly sand the edges of the cowboy hat, the star, and the snakes. Using a clean, damp cloth, wipe the dust from the wood shapes.

5 Using a glue gun, attach the silver feathers to the left side of the hat band. Attach the star on top of the silver feathers at the end of the hat band. Refer to the photograph for suggested placement.

6 Using clear matte spray finish, spray the cowboy hat and the snakes. Apply a second coat of spray finish to the cowboy hat and snakes. Let the spray finish dry between coats.

7 Using the glue gun, attach the cowboy hat and the snakes to the chair. Refer to the photograph for suggested placement.

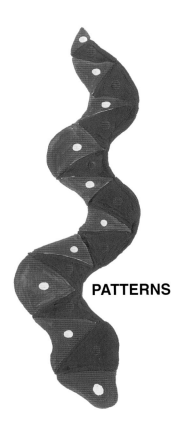

PATTERNS

THINGS YOU'LL NEED:

For the Cow Chair:

Miniature grapevine chair,
  11" tall with a
  4¹/₂" x 4¹/₂" seat
Cow,
  4" x 6" x ¹/₈" balsa wood
Presealed canvas,
  12" x 12" or 5" x 18"
1" Beige fringe, 1 yard
Straight pins
Beige thread
Pencil
Tracing paper
Graphite paper
¹/₂" Flat brush
Small pointed brush
Acrylic paint:
  Azalea blush
  Baby blue
  Baby pink
  Lavender
  Moon yellow
  Pale green
  White
Medium-point permanent
  black marker
Glue gun and glue sticks
Clear matte spray finish
Cotton batting, 4¹/₄" x 4¹/₄"
Cotton fabric, 4¹/₄" x 4¹/₄"

FOLLOW THESE STEPS:

1 Cut the cow from the ¹/₈" balsa wood. Use the cow pattern from page 47. Refer to the General Instructions for transferring patterns.

2 Using a ¹/₂" flat brush, paint one side and all the edges of the cow with white acrylic paint. Let the paint dry.

3 Using a pencil, draw small circles (flowers) on the cow. Refer to the pattern.

4 From the presealed canvas, cut one 4¹/₄" x 4¹/₄" square. Using the pencil, trace the seat cushion pattern and the rug pattern from below and page 47 onto tracing paper. Using graphite paper, transfer the patterns onto the 4¹/₄" x 4¹/₄" square piece of presealed canvas and the remaining piece of presealed canvas. Refer to the pattern.

5 Because you will be using small quantities of acrylic paint, it is easier to paint all three pieces at once. Using a small pointed brush, start by painting the flowers, then paint the petals. Let the paint dry. Refer to the patterns for suggested colors for painting.

6 Using a medium-point permanent black marker, outline the flowers, the leaves, and the borders.

Add small dots as shown on the patterns.

7 Using clear matte spray finish, spray the canvas. Spray the cow and let the spray finish dry. Apply a second coat of spray finish to the cow. Let the spray finish dry.

8 Using straight pins, pin the fringe to the front side of the rug. Using beige thread, topstitch the fringe in place. Place the cotton batting between the wrong side of the canvas and the wrong side of the cotton fabric. Sew the fabric and the canvas together using a ¹/₈" seam allowance.

9 Using a glue gun, attach the cow to the chair. Refer to the photograph for suggested placement. If preferred, permanently attach the cushion to the chair's seat.

PATTERN

46

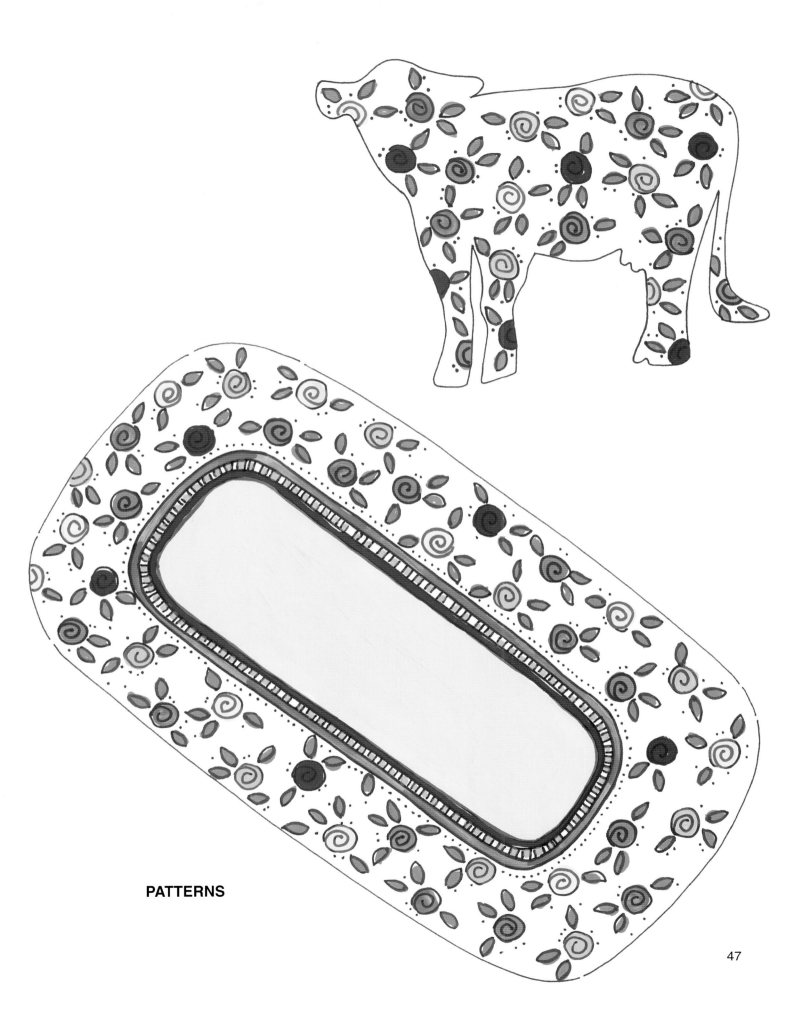

PATTERNS

47

Idea: A watermelon back with a matching chair pad... or put a Santa face and a

snowman on your chair for a holiday flair!

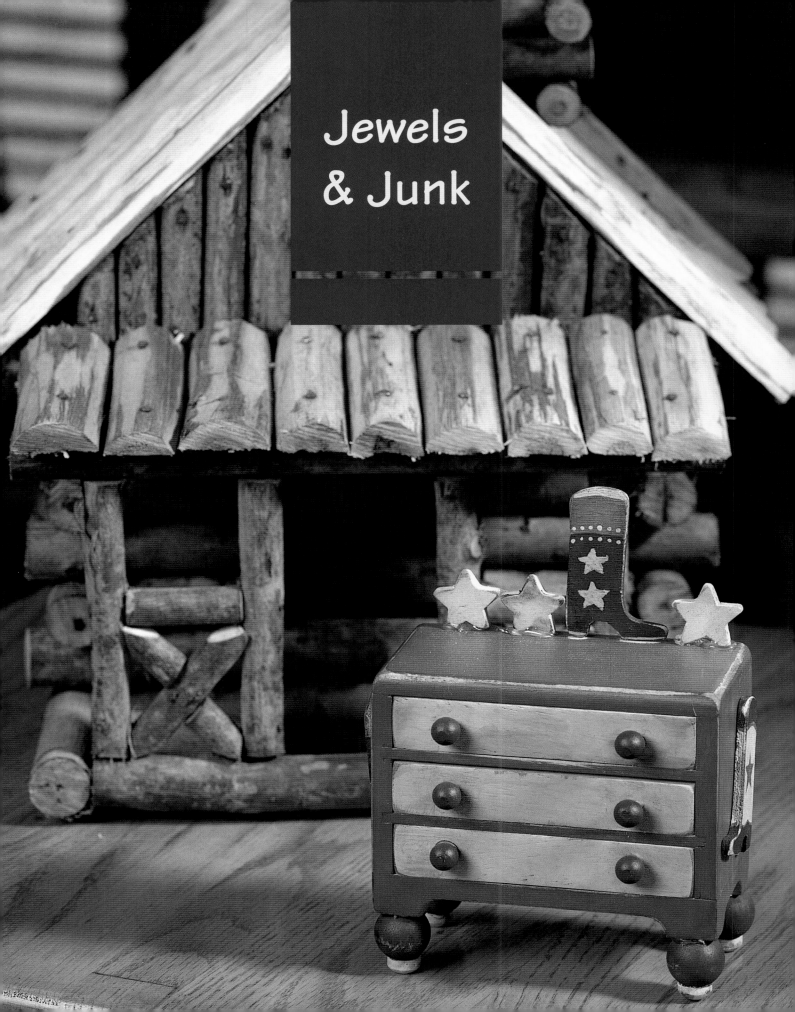

Jewels
& Junk

Jewels & Junk

I don't wear a lot of jewelry, but occasionally I will wear small pierced earrings. I thought this little miniature chest of drawers would be an ideal piece to house my small earrings. I have a small jewelry box in our home in Utah, so this one will sit on the bed table in our ranch house in Wyoming.

THINGS YOU'LL NEED:

Wooden doll furniture
  chest of drawers,
  unfinished or with only
  a clear varnish,
  2" deep x 2³/₄" high x
  3³/₄" wide with 3 drawers
3 Stars,
  4" x 2" x ¹/₈" balsa wood
3 Boots,
  5" x 3" x ¹/₈" balsa wood
6 Wooden beads,
  ¹/₂" diameter
4 Wooden beads,
  ⁵/₈" diameter
4 Wooden plugs, ³/₈"
2 Pair of pliers
Pencil
¹/₄" Flat brush
1" Sponge brush
Small pointed brush
Spackling compound
Fine-grit sandpaper
Medium-grit sandpaper
Clean cloth

Acrylic paint:
  Brilliant blue
  Calico red
  Moon yellow
Oil paint:
  Burnt umber
Mineral spirits
Rag or old cloth
Glue gun and glue sticks
  or Tacky glue
Clear matte spray finish

FOLLOW THESE STEPS:

1 Cut the stars and the boots from the ¹/₈" balsa wood. Use the patterns from page 51. Refer to the General Instructions for transferring patterns.

2 Using medium-grit sand-paper, lightly sand the chest of drawers. If the chest of drawers has a clear var-nish on it, sand until acrylic paint will adhere to the sur-faces. Remove the drawers from the chest. Remove any knobs from the drawers and discard them.

3 Using a pair of pliers, grab one wooden plug at the base where it flairs. With the second pair of pliers, break off the end of the dowel part of the plug. This will al-low it to fit nicely into one of the ⁵/₈" wooden beads to cre-ate the legs. Repeat the process for the remaining wooden plugs. Place hot glue or Tacky glue inside one ⅝" wooden bead hole and insert a wooden plug. Hold in place until secure. Repeat the process for the remaining beads.

4 Using a ¼" flat brush, paint the chest of drawers with calico red acrylic paint. Apply as many coats as necessary to cover. Let the paint dry between coats. Paint the drawer fronts with moon yellow acrylic paint. Do not paint the sides or insides of the drawers because they will stick and not open properly. Paint the large ends of the wooden plugs with moon yellow acrylic paint. Paint both sides of the stars and all of the edges with moon yellow acrylic paint. Paint all wooden beads with brilliant blue acrylic paint. As you paint the chest of drawers, the drawer fronts, and the wooden beads, paint the boots with a small pointed brush. Be sure to paint only one side and all of the edges of the boots. Refer to the patterns for suggested colors for painting. Using a pencil, draw the patterns on one side of the boots before painting. Let the paint dry between coats.

5 Using your finger, spackle the holes of the wooden beads with spackling compound. Using a clean, damp cloth, wipe the excess spackling compound from the beads. Let the spackling compound dry completely.

6 Using fine-grit sandpaper, lightly sand the edges of the chest of drawers, the drawer fronts, the legs, the boots, and the stars. Using a clean, damp cloth, wipe the dust from the painted wood shapes.

7 Using a glue gun or Tacky glue, attach the beads to the drawer fronts. Refer to the photograph for suggested placement. Using a small pointed brush, touchup the spackling with brilliant blue acrylic paint on the front of the knobs. Let the paint dry. Attach the legs to each corner on the bottom of the chest of drawers. Attach one boot to each end of the chest of drawers. Attach the stars and the remaining boot to the top back side of the chest of drawers. Hold in place until secure. Refer to the photograph for suggested placement.

8 Mix 1 part of burnt umber oil paint to 3 parts of mineral spirits. Using a 1" sponge brush, paint this stain over the chest of drawers, the drawer fronts, the legs, the boots, and the stars. Let the stain dry for about 15 to 20 seconds and, using a rag or old cloth, wipe off the remaining stain.

9 Remove the drawers from the chest of drawers. Using clear matte spray finish, spray the chest of drawers, the drawers, the boots, and the stars. Apply a second coat of spray finish to the chest of drawers, drawers, boots, and stars. Let the spray finish dry between coats and insert the drawers.

Idea: You choose three from five designs

PATTERNS

51

A Holder with a Heart

It was fun to use a wooden object made for a sole purpose and turn it into something else. This was the first time I had ever used a rubber stamp and I was amazed at how well stamping worked with acrylic paint.

THINGS YOU'LL NEED:

Wooden tissue box holder,
  5" wide x 5³/₄" tall
4 Wooden finials,
  1¹/₂" diameter x 2" tall
Heart, rubber stamp or
  stencil, 1¹/₄" square
Ruler
Pencil
¹/₂" Flat brush
1" Sponge brush
Small pointed brush
Stencil brush, if stenciling
Fine-grit sandpaper
Clean cloth
Acrylic paint:
  Butter pecan
  Thicket green
Oil paint:
  Burnt umber
Mineral spirits
Rag or old cloth
Old toothbrush
Glue gun and glue sticks
Clear matte spray finish

FOLLOW THESE STEPS:

1 Turn the tissue box holder upside down so the hole is on the bottom. Starting at the bottom, measure 1⁵/₈" squares—three across, three high—with a ruler and mark with a pencil. The middle squares may be slightly larger. Leave a ⁵/₈" border at the top. Using the pencil, draw three inverted triangles above each square on the ⁵/₈"

border—nine inverted triangles on each side. Refer to Diagram A. Draw the inverted triangles on the remaining sides.

2 Using a 1" sponge brush, paint the inside and the edges of the tissue box holder with thicket green acrylic paint. Paint the wooden finials, which will be used as the planter's legs, with thicket green acrylic paint. Using a ¹/₂" flat brush, paint all of the "tan" squares with butter pecan acrylic paint. Refer to Diagram A. Paint the remaining squares with thicket green acrylic paint. Let the paint dry between coats. Don't worry about uneven lines; if a small amount of wood shows through between the paint, it will absorb the stain you will apply later and will enhance the project.

3 Using a small pointed brush, paint all of the bottom triangles with butter pecan acrylic paint. Paint all of the upper triangles with thicket green acrylic paint. Add dots of thicket green acrylic paint to the butter pecan colored triangles. Add dots of butter pecan acrylic paint to the thicket green colored triangles. Let the paint dry between coats. Refer to the photograph for suggested placement.

4 If you are using a rubber stamp, apply acrylic paint to the rubber stamp using the 1/2" flat brush. You will need to apply acrylic paint to the rubber stamp before stamping each square. Stamp all of the butter pecan colored squares on all four sides of the tissue box holder with a thicket green colored heart. Stamp all of the thicket green colored squares on all four sides of the tissue box holder with a butter pecan colored heart. If

you are using a stencil, repeat the same color pattern as described. Press the stencil against each square before you apply acrylic paint with a stencil brush. Refer to the General Instructions for stenciling.

5 Using fine-grit sandpaper, lightly sand all the edges of the wooden finials. Using a clean, damp cloth, wipe the dust from the legs.

6 Mix 1 part of burnt umber oil paint to 4 parts of mineral spirits. Using the 1" sponge brush, paint this stain over the tissue box holder and the wooden finials. Let the stain dry for about 20 to 30 seconds and, using a rag or old cloth, wipe off the remaining stain. Leave the stain in the grooves. Apply more burnt umber color to the butter pecan colored areas than to the thicket green colored areas.

7 Using a glue gun, attach one wooden finial to each corner on the top of the tissue box holder (which is now the bottom). Hold in place until se-

cure. Refer to the photograph for suggested placement.

8 Dip an old toothbrush into the burnt umber oil paint / mineral spirits stain. Using your finger, "flip" the mixture onto the tissue box holder from a distance of about six inches. Using this technique, paint the tissue box holder on all sides. Refer to the General Instructions for painting with a toothbrush. Let the stain dry.

9 Using clear matte spray finish, spray the tissue box holder. Apply a second coat of spray finish to the tissue box holder. Make sure the inside of the tissue box holder is well coated with spray finish to repel water. Let the spray finish dry between coats. The hole in the bottom of the tissue box holder will allow water to run through the plant and not accumulate in the "planter." Plant your favorite flower in a clay pot and place the clay pot inside the planter. It is recommended that this "planter" be used indoors.

DIAGRAM A

Peek-
a-Boo

Peek-a-Boo

I bought a ceramic mirror in Park City, Utah, over twenty years ago that had one little bird perched looking into the bottom of the mirror. When I saw these little birds on a wire, I knew they would work for me in using the concept to create my own design. The mirror is just the right size to see if you have birdseed in your teeth!

THINGS YOU'LL NEED:

Wooden frame,
  9$\frac{1}{2}$" square
  with 4$\frac{1}{2}$"-square opening
Mirror, 5" x 5" square
2 Wooden birds with wire
  attached to the bottom,
  2$\frac{1}{2}$" long x 1" high
  x $\frac{3}{4}$" deep
Miniature Americana
  window shutters,
  4$\frac{1}{2}$" long x 1$\frac{1}{4}$" wide
4 Variegated
  green / rust beads, $\frac{1}{2}$"
$\frac{1}{2}$" Flat brush
1" Sponge brush
Small pointed brush
Spackling knife or metal ruler
Spackling compound
Fine-grit sandpaper
Clean cloth

Acrylic paint:
  Barnyard red
  Black
  Mint green
  Mustard
  White
Oil paint:
  Burnt umber
Mineral spirits
Rag or old cloth
Glue gun and glue sticks
Clear matte spray finish
Masking tape or
  small brad nails
  and hammer

FOLLOW THESE STEPS:

1 Using either a spackling knife or a metal ruler, spackle the wooden frame with spackling compound. Refer to the General Instructions for spackling and texturing techniques. Let the spackling compound dry completely.

2 Using fine-grit sandpaper, lightly sand all spackled surfaces. Using a clean, damp cloth, wipe the dust from the frame.

3 Using a 1" sponge brush, paint over parts of the spackled side of the frame and the edges with mint green acrylic paint. Refer to Diagram A. Repeat this process using white acrylic paint. Allow some of the raw wood to remain exposed.

4 Using the ¹/₂" flat brush, paint one bird with barnyard red acrylic paint. Paint the second bird with mustard acrylic paint. Using a small pointed brush, paint the birds' eyes with black acrylic paint. Paint the barnyard red colored bird's beak with mustard acrylic paint. Paint the mustard colored bird's beak with black acrylic paint.

5 Mix 1 part of burnt umber oil paint to 4 parts of mineral spirits. Using the 1" sponge brush, paint this stain over

the frame and sides. Let the stain dry for about 30 seconds and, using a rag or old cloth, wipe off the remaining stain. If the frame is too dark, wipe it with mineral spirits to lighten. Repeat this process on the birds.

6 Using a glue gun, glue the wire on the bottom of the barnyard red colored bird down one side of the frame— under where the shutter is to be placed. Leave enough wire so that the bird can bend to look

inside the mirror that will be placed in the frame. Glue the wire on the bottom of the second bird from the opposite corner up. Attach one shutter over the top of each wire, aligning the edge with the inside edge of the frame. Hold in place until secure. Attach the beads. Refer to the photograph for suggested placement.

7 Using clear matte spray finish, spray the frame and the birds. Apply a second coat of spray finish to the frame and birds. Let the spray finish dry between coats.

8 Insert the mirror in the frame and secure with masking tape or small brad nails hammered into the sides of the frame.

Idea: Use a doll house window over the mirror or a photograph instead of shutters...the birds will still be able to see inside...

DIAGRAM A

57

Buttons
Add Dimension

This was originally designed to be a pillow top, and it would adapt to canvas very nicely. I just redecorated my bedroom in Utah with black, taupe, tan, and a touch of rust. This design was stimulated by that color combination. I think the wooden buttons add a dimension to the picture that I really like. Who knows, maybe this will end up in my bedroom?

THINGS YOU'LL NEED:

Wooden frame,
    20" x 20" x 14"
    with 14" opening
14" x 14" x $1/4$" pine
4 Wooden buttons
    in each size,
    $1/2$", $3/4$", $7/8$", and 1"
Ruler
Pencil
Tracing paper
Graphite paper
Masking tape
$1/4$" Flat brush
Acrylic paint:
    Acorn brown
    Butter pecan
    Linen beige
    Wrought iron black
Textured rag
Paper towels
Medium-point
    permanent black marker
Clear matte spray finish
Matching thread and needle
Glue gun and glue sticks

FOLLOW THESE STEPS:

1 Using a ruler and a pencil, measure and draw a 12" x 12" square on the 14" square of pine. Measure a $1/4$" border inside the 12" square. Draw a $9/2$" x $9/2$" square on the pine using the border. Continue the lines to meet the 12" square at the corners. Refer to Diagram A. In the $1/4$" border area, draw a vertical line from each square you created at the corners. Then add perpen-

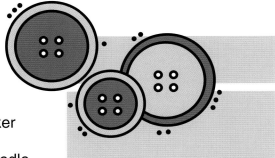

dicular lines to create smaller squares. Draw 12 rows of squares on each side. Do not use a ruler for this step, as it doesn't matter if the squares are perfectly square. They will be more appealing if they vary slightly in size. Refer to Diagram A.

2 Using the pencil, trace the heart pattern from page 60 onto tracing paper. Using graphite paper, transfer the pattern onto the $1/4$" pine, centering it in the middle of the design.

3 Using a $1/4$" flat brush, paint the 1" border and the area around the heart with wrought iron black acrylic paint. Using masking tape, cover the $1/4$" area between the painted areas and around the outside edges of the wrought iron black acrylic paint. Tape around the outside edges of the heart. The tape will crease to go around the rounded edges of the heart.

4 Dip the textured rag into the linen beige acrylic paint. Dab it onto a paper towel, then onto the wrought iron black painted areas. Leave room in between "dabs" because you will be adding another color. Dip the textured rag into the butter pecan acrylic paint and repeat the process. Let the paint dry between coats. Refer to the photograph for reference. Remove the masking tape.

5 Using the 1/4" flat brush, paint the heart with butter pecan acrylic paint. Paint the corner squares in the 1 1/4"

area with butter pecan acrylic paint. Don't worry about full coverage; brush strokes enhance the look. Starting at one corner with the small squares, paint alternating squares with butter pecan acrylic paint. Paint the remaining small squares with linen beige acrylic paint. Let the paint dry between coats.

6 Paint the inside top of each button with acorn brown acrylic paint. Paint the outside rim of each button with linen beige acrylic paint. Let the paint dry between coats.

7 Using a medium-point permanent black marker, make small dots around the inside edge of the acorn brown acrylic paint on the 1" wooden buttons. Refer to

Diagram B. Using the permanent black marker, outline the heart just inside the painted edge. Outline the squares around the heart just inside the painted edge. Draw double lines between the small painted squares. Randomly add small black dots to the small squares and the large corner squares. Refer to the photograph for suggested placement.

8 Using clear matte spray finish, spray the 1/4" pine and the buttons. Let the spray finish dry.

9 Using matching thread and a needle, sew through all the button holes. Using a glue gun, attach the buttons to the pine. Refer to Diagram A for suggested placement.

DIAGRAM A

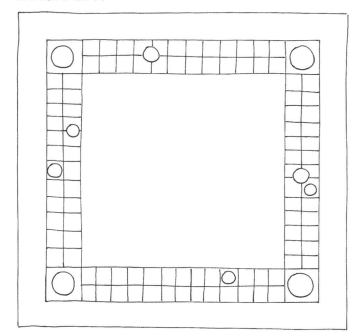

PATTERN
ENLARGE 180%

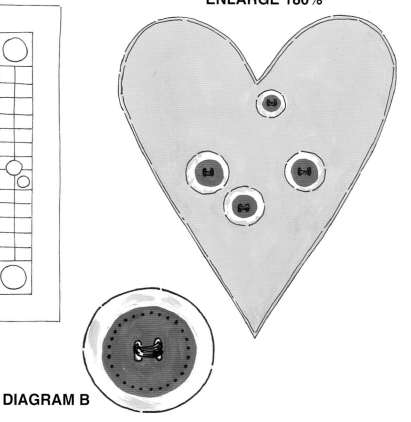

DIAGRAM B

Eiteljorg Museum
of American Indian and Western Art
Indianapolis, Indiana

Pastel
Apples

Pastel Apples

Roses are red, Violets are blue, Apples are anything ... except pastel blue! I am usually drawn to earth colors or vibrant primary colors, but when I bought these wooden apples, I just wanted to paint them in pastel colors. They will look good in my new green hutch in my Utah kitchen.

THINGS YOU'LL NEED:

Wooden bowl,
  6³/₄" diameter
6 Wooden apples,
  2¹/₂" diameter
Ruler
Pencil
¹/₂" Flat brush
Medium-grit sandpaper
Clean cloth
Acrylic paint:
  Butter pecan
  Lavender
  Mint green
  Pink
  Salmon
  White
  Yellow
Fine-point permanent
  gold marker
Clear matte spray finish

FOLLOW THESE STEPS:

1 Using medium-grit sandpaper, lightly sand the wooden bowl and the apples to remove any varnish or residue. Using a clean, damp cloth, wipe the dust from the bowl and the apples.

2 Using a ¹/₂" flat brush, paint the outside of the wooden bowl with white acrylic paint. Paint the inside and the top rim of the bowl with white acrylic paint. Let the paint dry between coats.

Apply additional coats of white acrylic paint until full coverage is achieved.

3 Using the ¹/₂" flat brush, paint one apple with salmon acrylic paint, one with pink acrylic paint, one with butter pecan acrylic paint, one with lavender acrylic paint, one with yellow acrylic paint, and the last one with mint green acrylic paint. Apply additional coats of acrylic paint until full coverage is achieved. Let the paint dry between coats.

4 Using a fine-point permanent gold marker, paint all of the apple stems. Draw each pattern onto each apple. Try to space the designs evenly over the entire apple. Be careful not to touch the wet marker as you draw. Refer to Diagram A for pattern choices.

5 Using a ruler and a pencil, draw a line ¼" down from the top edge of the bowl. Draw triangles in this space around the bowl. Do not use a ruler for this step, as it doesn't matter if the triangles are perfectly even. They will be more appealing if they vary slightly in size. Refer to Diagram B. Draw the same triangles on the top rim of the bowl.

6 Using the fine-point permanent gold marker, outline all of the triangles and add lines in the triangles. Add small dots inside the bowl rim. Let the marker dry. Refer to Diagram B.

7 Using clear matte spray finish, spray the bowl and the apples. To get full coverage on the apples, spray half of the apple, let the spray finish dry, turn it over and spray the remaining part of the apple. Apply a second coat of spray finish to the bowl and apples. Let the spray finish dry between coats.

DIAGRAM B

DIAGRAM A

Idea: We added a few more patterns

63

What to Do with Ugly Fruit

Everywhere you shop, it seems you run into ugly wooden fruits and vegetables! I took some of these, painted them, and made this whimsical box. This project is quite different from the rest. I just kept changing things and experimenting until I got something I liked. It was the first time I had ever used spray glitter on anything.

THINGS YOU'LL NEED:

Round bentwood box with lid,
    6" diameter x 3" high
6 Wooden balls, 1"
4 Wooden pears,
    1¹/₂" diameter
    (large end) x 2" tall
2 Wooden apples with stems,
    2" x 2" round
3 Silk leaves
Measuring tape
Pencil
¹/₂" Flat brush
Acrylic paint:
    Barnyard red
    Lavender
    Light gray
    Moon yellow
    White
    Wrought iron black
Gold spray glitter
Glue gun and glue sticks

FOLLOW THESE STEPS:

1 Using a ¹/₂" flat brush, paint the inside and the outside of the round bentwood box and lid with white acrylic paint. Paint the rim of the lid with moon yellow acrylic paint. Apply only one coat of acrylic paint to the bentwood box and lid. Paint the fruits: 1" wooden balls with lavender acrylic paint, wooden pears with moon yellow acrylic paint, wooden apples with barnyard red acrylic paint, and the apple stems with wrought iron black acrylic paint. Apply additional coats of acrylic paint until full coverage is achieved. Let the paint dry between coats.

2 Using a measuring tape, measure around the bottom of the box. Using a pencil, mark at each ¹/₂". Add ¹/₂" marks all the way to the top of the box. Any discrepancy in the width of the last ¹/₂" mark will be covered by the lid. Without using a ruler, draw vertical lines from the top marks to the bottom marks. Starting at the top of the box, measure down ¹/₂" three times. Using the pencil, mark these distances about four times around the box. Without using a ruler, draw a line from one ¹/₂" mark to the next, until you've drawn a

65

circle around the box. Repeat at each ½" mark. Refer to the photograph. Without using a ruler, draw squares on the lid ½" apart, starting from the center.

3 Using the ½" flat brush, paint alternating squares on the lid and the outside of the box with wrought iron black acrylic paint. Make only two brush strokes per square. Pull the brush down from one side; then turn and pull toward the brush stroke. The sides should be even with the outside edge of the brush. Apply only one coat of acrylic paint to these squares. Let the paint dry.

4 Without measuring, draw squares around the edge of the lid. Don't worry about

them being perfectly square. Paint the squares with barnyard red acrylic paint. Apply only one coat of acrylic paint to these squares. Paint diagonal lines over the edge of the barnyard red squares with moon yellow acrylic paint to create a diamond. Make sure the paint is thin so the barnyard red acrylic paint will show through the moon yellow acrylic paint and look almost gray. Refer to Diagram A. Let the paint dry between coats.

5 Dry-brush the pears, apples, and lavender balls (grapes) with light gray acrylic paint. Refer to the General Instructions for dry brushing.

6 Using the pencil, draw a 4" square on the bottom of the box. Using a glue gun, attach one pear (with the small part of the pear to the box) to each corner of the 4" square. The pears will be the legs on the box.

7 Using the glue gun, attach the apples, the grapes, and the leaves to the top of the lid. Refer to the photograph for placement.

8 Using gold spray glitter, spray the inside and the outside of the box and lid. Let the spray glitter dry.

DIAGRAM A

Idea: Replace the fruit with these...

- Birds & Nests
- Painted Blocks
- Easter Eggs
- Assorted Veggies
- Houses & Trees
- Zoo Animals

Something
Fishy

Something Fishy

The fish pictured around the frame are actually ornaments. The frame was designed and colored around these ornaments. I found the old handle in our machinery shed at the ranch and couldn't resist incorporating it into this piece. I am a nut about weathered metal and this handle added a unique dimension to the frame.

THINGS YOU'LL NEED:

Wooden frame,
   9¹/₂" square
   with 4¹/₂" square opening
3 Wooden fish,
   8" x 24" x ¹/₂" pine
8 Clay beads, 1" square
Metal handle,
   rusted or painted black,
   7³/₄" long (end to end) x
   1" wide x 2" high with
   2" base
¹/₂" Flat brush
1" Sponge brush
Small pointed brush
Carving knife or
   heavy-duty X-acto knife
Spackling knife or metal ruler
Spackling compound
Fine-grit sandpaper
Medium-grit sandpaper
Clean cloth

Acrylic paint:
   Acorn brown
   Mustard
   Sedona clay
   Wrought iron black
Oil paint:
   Burnt umber
Mineral spirits
Rag or old cloth
Glue gun and glue sticks
Clear matte spray finish

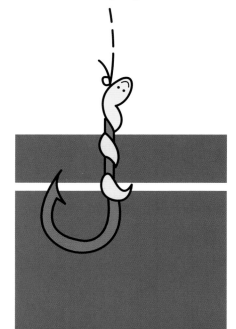

FOLLOW THESE STEPS:

1 Cut the fish from the ¹/₂" pine. Use the fish pattern from page 69. Refer to the General Instructions for transferring patterns.

2 Using a carving knife or a heavy-duty X-acto knife, score the gills and tail according to the pattern. Using medium-grit sandpaper, lightly sand the fish until the edges are smooth. Using a clean, damp cloth, wipe the dust from the fish.

3 Using a ¹/₂" flat brush, paint the fish with mustard acrylic paint. Dry-brush the upper part of the fish with wrought iron black acrylic paint. Dry-brush the bottom part of the fish with Sedona clay acrylic paint. Dry-brush the entire fish with acorn brown acrylic paint. Let the paint dry between coats. Refer to the General Instructions for dry brushing.

4 Using either a spackling knife or a metal ruler, spackle one side and all of the edges of the frame with spackling compound. Refer to the General Instructions for spackling and texturing techniques. Let the spackling compound dry completely.

5 Using fine-grit sandpaper, lightly sand all spackled and textured surfaces. Using a clean, damp cloth, wipe the dust from the frame.

6 Using the ½" flat brush, paint the spackled side and all edges of the frame with Sedona clay and mustard acrylic paints. Refer to Diagram A. Leave some of the raw wood exposed—do not paint. Dry-brush the

entire frame with acorn brown acrylic paint. Let the paint dry between coats. Refer to the General Instructions for dry brushing.

7 Mix 1 part of burnt umber oil paint to 5 parts of mineral spirits. Using a 1" sponge brush, paint this stain over the frame. Let the stain dry for about 30 seconds and, using a rag or old cloth, wipe off the remaining stain.

8 Using a small pointed brush, touchup the spackling with burnt umber oil paint. Let the paint dry. Using a glue gun, glue the fish to

the sides of the frame. Glue the clay beads to the front of the frame. Refer to the photograph for suggested placement. Using hot glue, glue the metal handle to the bottom side of the frame. Hold in place until secure.

9 Using clear matte spray finish, spray the front and the edges of the frame, the fish, and the handle. Apply a second coat of spray finish to the frame, fish, and handle. Let the spray finish dry between coats before placing a photograph or mirror in the opening.

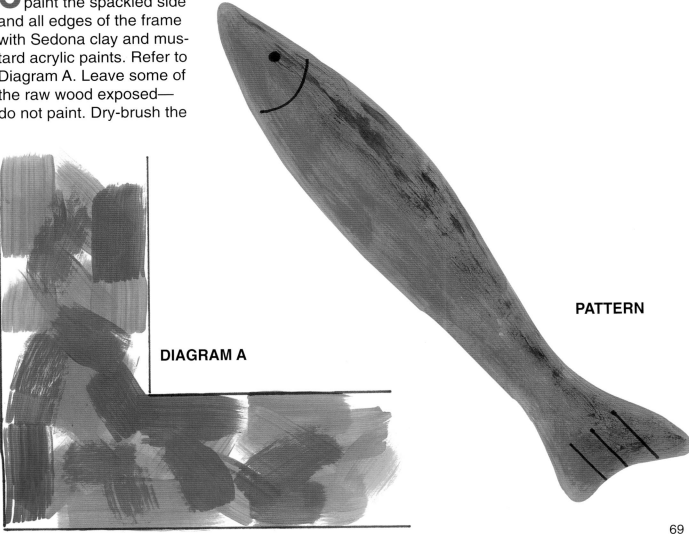

DIAGRAM A

PATTERN

Oh Nuts

I wanted to create a large project for this book, but have it be simple enough to create in an afternoon. My stepdaughter, Marni, was visiting our ranch when I made this mirror. She loved it and I told her she could have it. She decided she'd rather try to make one of her own — she'll be a good barometer on how well I did ....

THINGS YOU'LL NEED:

Wooden frame with
  beveled mirror,
  15$\frac{1}{4}$" x 19"
  (9$\frac{3}{4}$" x 13$\frac{1}{2}$" mirror)
12 Leaves,
  4" x 24" x $\frac{1}{8}$" balsa wood
12 Acorns,
  4" x 12" x $\frac{1}{8}$" balsa wood
Newspaper
Masking tape
$\frac{1}{2}$" Flat brush
1" Sponge brush
Fine-grit sandpaper
Clean cloth

Acrylic paint:
  Acorn brown
  Avocado green
  Linen beige
  Mustard
  Sedona clay
Oil paint:
  Burnt umber
Mineral spirits
Rag or old cloth
Old toothbrush
Fine-point permanent
  black marker
Glue gun and glue sticks
Clear matte spray finish

FOLLOW THESE STEPS:

1 Cut the leaves and the acorns from the $\frac{1}{8}$" balsa wood. Use the leaves and acorn patterns from page 72. Refer to the General Instructions for transferring patterns. Using fine-grit sandpaper, lightly sand the edges of the leaves and acorns until they are smooth. Using a clean, damp cloth, wipe the dust from the leaves and acorns.

2 Using newspaper, cover the beveled mirror. Using masking tape, tape the newspaper to the inside edges of the wooden frame.

3 Using a $\frac{1}{2}$" flat brush, paint the wooden frame with linen beige acrylic paint. If the frame has an inside edge, paint the edge with Sedona clay acrylic paint.

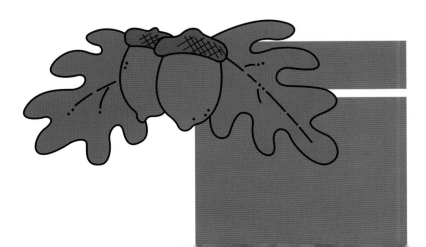

4 Mix 1 part of burnt umber oil paint to 3 parts of mineral spirits. Dip an old toothbrush into this stain. Using your finger, "flip" the mixture onto the frame from a distance of about six inches. Using this technique, paint the frame on all sides. Refer to the General Instructions for painting with a toothbrush. Let the stain dry for about 5 minutes. Using a 1" sponge brush, paint the entire frame with this stain. Let the stain dry for about 30 seconds and, using a rag or old cloth, wipe off the remaining stain, being careful not to remove the "toothbrush" spatters.

5 Using the 1/2" flat brush, paint four leaves with Sedona clay acrylic paint. Paint four leaves with mustard acrylic paint. Paint four leaves with avocado green acrylic paint. Use broad paint strokes and leave part of the raw wood exposed. Paint only one side of the leaves, but paint all of their edges. Let the paint dry. Paint all of the acorns with acorn brown acrylic paint. Use broad paint strokes and leave part of the raw wood exposed. Paint only one side of the acorns, but paint all of their edges. Let the paint dry. Refer to patterns.

6 Dry-brush all of the leaves with acorn brown acrylic paint. Let the paint dry. Refer to the General Instructions for dry brushing.

7 Mix 1 part of burnt umber oil paint to 3 parts of mineral spirits. Using the 1" sponge brush, paint the leaves and the acorns with this stain. Let the stain dry for about 30 seconds and, using a rag or old cloth, wipe off the remaining stain. Let the stain dry completely. Using a fine-point permanent black marker, draw the details on the acorns. Refer to the pattern.

8 Using a glue gun, attach the leaves and the acorns to the frame. Refer to the photograph for suggested placement.

9 Using clear matte spray finish, spray the entire frame, the leaves, and the acorns. Apply two additional coats of spray finish to the frame, leaves, and acorns. Let the spray finish dry between coats. Remove the masking tape and the newspaper from the mirror.

PATTERN

Idea: How about a Lily and a leaf for a spring mirror? Try these patterns

Mr.
Fish

Mr. Fish

This project was actually made by my friend, Jo Packham. It hangs above her kitchen window. When I saw the fish, I loved it, and asked if I could include it in my book. She has a marvelous sense of design and can put colors together better than anyone I know. I think this piece is reflective of that talent.

THINGS YOU'LL NEED:

24" x 12" x ³/₄" pine
Gold-leaf adhesive
1 Package gold leaf
Clean rag
1" Sponge brush
Medium pointed brush
Textured sponge
Fine-grit sandpaper
Clean cloth
Acrylic paint:
  Aqua
  Blue
  Gold
  Lavender
  Linen beige
  Olive green
  Pink
  Sedona clay
  Yellow
Oil paint:
  Burnt umber
Rag or old cloth
Clear matte spray finish

FOLLOW THESE STEPS:

1 Cut the fish from the ³/₄" pine. Use the fish pattern from page 75. Refer to the General Instructions for transferring patterns.

2 Using fine-grit sandpaper, lightly sand the edges of the fish until they are smooth. Using a clean, damp cloth, wipe the dust from the fish.

3 Using a 1" sponge brush, paint the fish with aqua acrylic paint. Using a textured sponge, sponge the acrylic paints onto the fish. Start with

the darkest color and continue to the lightest color. Refer to the pattern. Let the paint dry between coats. Refer to the General Instructions for sponge painting.

4 Using a medium pointed brush, draw swirls on the body of the fish with gold, olive green, and Sedona clay acrylic paints and the dots with Sedona clay acrylic paint. Let the paint dry between coats. Refer to the pattern for suggested placement.

5 Using a 1" sponge brush, apply gold-leaf adhesive to the nose and the tail sections of the fish. Let the adhesive dry until it feels tacky to the touch. Apply the gold leaf onto the tacky adhesive. Don't worry about full coverage. Using a clean rag, wipe over the gold leaf to flatten and secure it.

6 Using a rag or old cloth, rub burnt umber oil paint over the gold leaf and carefully wipe it. Refer to the General Instructions for antiquing.

7 Using clear matte spray finish, spray the front and the sides of the fish. Apply a second coat of spray finish to the fish. Let the spray finish dry between coats.

PATTERNS

ENLARGE 200%

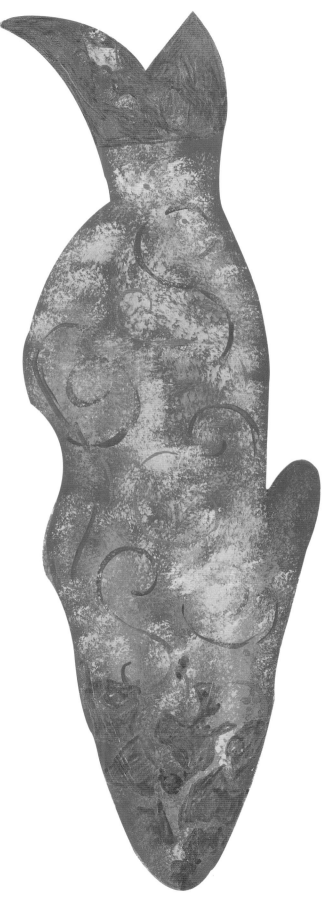

God Loves All Creatures

Since we own an excursion train in Clarkdale, Arizona, we spend a great deal of time in the Southwest. I am always inspired by the Southwest coloring and design. This simple frame and mat was made after a trip to Sedona. My sister, Nan, always reminds me of our link with God, so the saying was inspired by her.

THINGS YOU'LL NEED:

Wooden frame,
 12" x 15^1/$_2$" x ^{3}/$_4$" with
 double mat,
 white or off-white,
 (3^3/$_4$" x 4^3/$_4$" opening)
Ruler
Pencil
Tracing paper
Graphite paper
Small pointed brush
Medium-grit sandpaper
Clean cloth

Acrylic paint:
 Butterscotch
 Lavender
 Melon
 Plantation green
Fine-point permanent
 gold marker
Clear matte spray finish
Laser paper, 8^1/$_2$" x 11
Cardboard, 8^1/$_2$" x 11
Color photocopy, 8^1/$_2$" x 11
Spray adhesive
Masking tape

FOLLOW THESE STEPS:

1 Remove the backing, the mat, and the glass from the frame. Using medium-grit sandpaper, lightly sand the frame. Using a clean, damp cloth, wipe the dust from the frame.

2 Hold a ruler at the edge of the frame and, using a pencil, draw freehanded triangles ^{1}/$_2$" apart. Draw another triangle inside each of the first triangles. Refer to Diagram A.

3 Using the pencil, draw squares at the corners of the opening of the mat. Refer to Diagram B. Using the pencil, trace the rabbit pattern from page 78 onto tracing paper. Using graphite paper, transfer the rabbit pattern onto the mat so that the bot-

77

tom of the rabbit is along the square. Center the rabbit on each side. Refer to the photograph for suggested placement.

4 Using a small pointed brush, paint one section on the frame, one square, and one rabbit at a time. Let the paint dry after each color. Refer to the pattern for suggested colors for painting.

5 Using a fine-point permanent gold marker, outline all the squares, rabbits, and

the pattern colors on the frame. Don't worry about the lines being even, if they fluctuate in size, especially around the rabbits, they will enhance the project.

6 Using clear matte spray finish, spray the frame and the mat. Apply a second coat of spray finish to the frame only. Let the spray finish dry between coats.

7 Center the saying: "God loves all creatures large and small" on the laser paper,

either handwritten or computer generated. Make a color photocopy that matches one of the colors on the frame. Using spray adhesive, attach the color photocopy cutout to the 8½" x 11 piece of cardboard. Place the glass and the mat in the frame. Center and mount the saying in the opening of the frame onto the back of the mat with masking tape.

DIAGRAM B

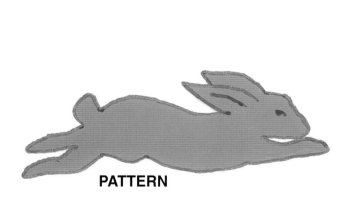

PATTERN

Idea: Put an ark, a pig or an exotic cat on the mat

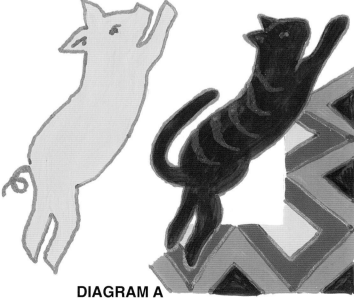

DIAGRAM A

Switch
One
Will You
Paint?

Switch One Will You Paint?

Without exception, almost every house has at least one light switch covered by a light switch plate. So often, they are located in simple spaces where no other decor can be hung. I think these are ideal two-hour projects and terrific for gifts. They are so simple and yet so noticeable when entering a room.

THINGS YOU'LL NEED:

Light switch plate with
   arched top to fit a
   single switch or
   4" x 7" x ¹/₈" balsa wood
3 Wooden houses,
   6" x 2" x ¹/₈" balsa wood
3 Wooden stars,
   1" x 3" x ¹/₈" balsa wood
Wooden moon,
   1³/₄" x 1¹/₂" x ¹/₈" balsa wood
Pencil
¹/₂" Flat brush
Small pointed brush
Fine-grit
   sandpaper
Clean cloth

Acrylic paint:
   Barnyard red
   Butter pecan
   Sedona clay
   Light mint
   Navy blue
   Plantation green
   Teddy bear tan
   Thicket green
   White
Glue gun and glue sticks
   or Tacky glue
Clear matte spray finish
Small blunt-end screws
   and screwdriver

FOLLOW THESE STEPS:

For the House Switch Plate:

1 Cut the light switch plate and the shapes from the ¹/₈" balsa wood. Use the patterns from page 81. Refer to the General Instructions for transferring patterns.

2 Using a pencil, draw windows and doors on the houses. Refer to the pattern. Draw hillsides on the light switch plate. Refer to the pattern.

3 Using a small pointed brush, paint the houses, doors, roofs, chimneys, and windows with acrylic paints. Let the paint dry between each color. Refer to the pattern for suggested colors for painting. Paint the moon with tan acrylic paint. Paint the stars with white acrylic paint. Let the paint dry between coats.

4 Using fine-grit sandpaper, lightly sand the edges of the houses, the stars, and the moon. Using a clean, damp cloth, wipe the dust from the wood shapes.

5 Using a ½" flat brush, paint the light switch plate with acrylic paint. Refer to the pattern for suggested colors for painting. Start painting at the top of the light switch plate and work toward the bottom. Let the paint dry between colors.

6 Using either a glue gun or Tacky glue, attach the houses, the stars, and the moon to the light switch plate. Refer to the pattern for suggested placement.

7 Using clear matte spray finish, spray the light switch plate. Apply a second coat of spray finish to the light switch plate. Let the spray finish dry between coats.

8 Using small blunt-end screws and a screwdriver, place the light switch plate in your favorite room!

Idea: New Patterns!

PATTERN

81

Reindeer on the Range

I liked this reindeer shape so well I used it on two different projects in this book. There is such freedom in its movement. We have a ranch in Wyoming and hundreds of whitetail and mule deer roam the meadows and mountain slopes. This reindeer reminds me of them. The frame has a Western flavor with the addition of the sisal on the frame.

THINGS YOU'LL NEED:

Wooden frame,
  6" x 7$\frac{1}{2}$" x $\frac{1}{4}$"
  with 3$\frac{1}{2}$" x 5" opening
Wooden reindeer,
  5$\frac{1}{2}$" x 5" x $\frac{1}{8}$" balsa wood
$\frac{1}{4}$" Sisal, 14 feet
$\frac{1}{2}$" Flat brush
1" Sponge brush
Acrylic paint:
  Acorn brown
  Sedona clay
  Turquoise
Oil paint:
  Burnt umber
Mineral spirits
Rag or old cloth
Glue gun and glue sticks
Clear matte spray finish

Tacky glue
Brown paper bag
Spray adhesive
Scissors
Masking tape
Spray bottle with warm water
Picture hanger or
  2" x 4" wooden block

FOLLOW THESE STEPS:

1 Cut the reindeer from the $\frac{1}{8}$" balsa wood. Use the reindeer pattern from page 84. Refer to the General Instructions for transferring patterns.

2 Using a $\frac{1}{2}$" flat brush, paint the middle of one side of the reindeer with turquoise acrylic paint by dabbing the paint. Repeat this process around the edges of the reindeer with Sedona clay acrylic paint. Refer to the pattern. Let the paint dry between coats.

3 Dry-brush over the turquoise and Sedona clay acrylic paint on the reindeer with acorn brown acrylic paint. Let the paint dry. Refer to the General Instructions for dry brushing.

4 Mix 1 part of burnt umber oil paint to 3 parts of mineral spirits. Using a 1" sponge brush, paint the front and the sides of the reindeer. Let the stain dry for about 30 seconds and, using a rag or old cloth, wipe off the remaining stain.

5 Using clear matte spray finish, spray the reindeer. Apply a second coat of spray finish to the reindeer. Let the spray finish dry between coats.

6 Using scissors, cut the brown paper bag to 7$\frac{1}{4}$" x 8$\frac{3}{4}$". Using spray adhesive, spray one side of the cut piece of paper bag and attach it to the front of the frame. From the center, cut to the inside corners. Fold to the back

and trim the edges so they do not overlap onto the sides. Clip the outside corners perpendicular to the corner and fold to the other side. Refer to Diagram A. Trim as necessary and press the cut piece of paper bag against the back of the wooden board.

7 Using a glue gun, on the front of the board starting at one corner, attach the sisal, moving from the outside edge of the board to the center around the frame's opening. End the sisal at the corner where you began. Refer to Diagram B.

8 Center the photograph or picture in the frame's opening and secure it onto the back with masking tape. Cut one 5" x 7$\frac{1}{4}$" piece from

the paper bag. Place Tacky glue around the edges and attach it to the back of the frame over the photograph and masking tape. After the glue has thoroughly dried, spray the back with warm water. Let the water dry. This allows the paper bag to shrink and tighten up nicely on the back.

9 Using the glue gun, attach the reindeer to the top front of the frame over the sisal. Attach a picture hanger to the back of the frame or glue a 2" x 4" wooden block onto the bottom back of the frame if you choose to have a standing frame.

DIAGRAM A

DIAGRAM B

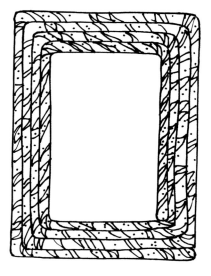

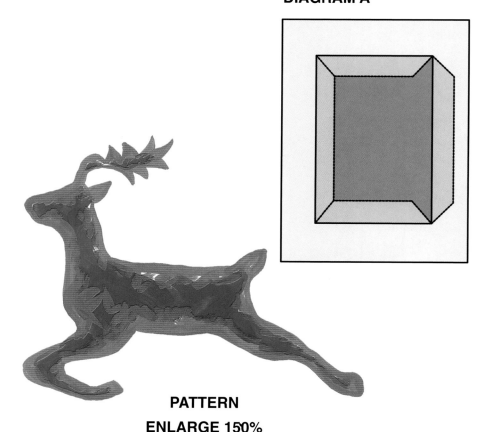

PATTERN

ENLARGE 150%

Ho
Ho Ho

Ho
Ho Ho

I still giggle when I look at this wooden stocking. I was proud of myself when I saw how animated these Santas became. I've used them in other mediums, but I liked seeing them translated to wood. I really got a kick out of carving the edges of so many of my pieces to make them look hand-carved. It actually looks like I knew what I was doing!

THINGS YOU'LL NEED:

8" x 20" x ³/₄" pine
2 Wooden stars,
   3" x 6" x ¹/₈" balsa wood
4 Wooden beads,
   ¹/₂" diameter
Pencil
Tracing paper
Graphite paper
¹/₂" Flat brush
Small pointed brush
1" Sponge brush
Carving knife or
   heavy-duty X-acto knife
Drill with ³/₁₆" drill bit

Acrylic paint:
   Barnyard red
   Butter pecan
   Butterscotch
   Christmas green
   White
Oil paint:
   Burnt umber
Mineral spirits
Rag or old cloth
Clear matte spray finish
Scissors
¹/₁₆" Rawhide leather,
   3 feet

FOLLOW THESE STEPS:

1 Cut the three pieces needed for the stocking from the ³/₄" pine and the stars from the ¹/₈" balsa wood. Use the stocking patterns from pages 87 and 88. Refer to the General Instructions for transferring patterns.

2 Using a carving knife or a heavy-duty X-acto knife, remove small pieces of wood from the edges of the wood shapes so they appear to have been hand-carved.

3 Using a drill with a ³/₁₆" drill bit, drill holes in all three wood pieces. Drill holes in the stars, off center. Refer to the pattern for suggested placement.

4 Using a pencil, trace the Santa pattern and the lettering from pages 87 and 88 onto tracing paper. Using

graphite paper, transfer the patterns onto the wooden shapes. Refer to the patterns for suggested placement. Using the pencil, draw small trees onto the stocking toe and heel.

5 Using a 1/2" flat brush and small pointed brush, paint the stocking with acrylic paints. Refer to the patterns for suggested colors for painting. Let the paint dry between coats. When painting, leave a small amount of wood exposed between all colors — even the dots on the treetops. When you stain over the painted pieces, the exposed wood will absorb more stain and act as an outline for the figures. The decorative lines around the Santas should be painted with barnyard red acrylic paint after the background and the Santas are painted. Don't worry about leaving space around them. Paint the wooden beads with one coat of barnyard red acrylic paint. Draw trees on both sides of the stars. Paint one side and all of the edges of the stars. Paint the other side of the star. Let the paint dry between coats.

6 Mix 1 part of burnt umber oil paint to 5 parts of mineral spirits. Using a 1" sponge brush, paint this stain over the front and sides of the stocking shapes, the stars, and the beads. Let the stain dry for about 30 seconds and, using a rag or old cloth, wipe off the remaining stain.

7 Using clear matte spray finish, spray the front and the sides of the stocking shapes, the stars, and the beads. Apply a second coat of spray finish to the stocking shapes, stars, and beads. Let the spray finish dry between coats.

8 Using scissors, cut the rawhide leader into four 6" lengths and one 12" length. Using two 6" lengths, tie the stocking toe to the stocking. Using the other two 6" lengths, tie the "Ho Ho Ho" strip to the top of the stocking. Knot the leather on the back side of the stocking. String the beads and the stars onto the remaining 12" leather strip. Attach it to the top of the stocking for hanging.

PATTERNS
ENLARGE 115%

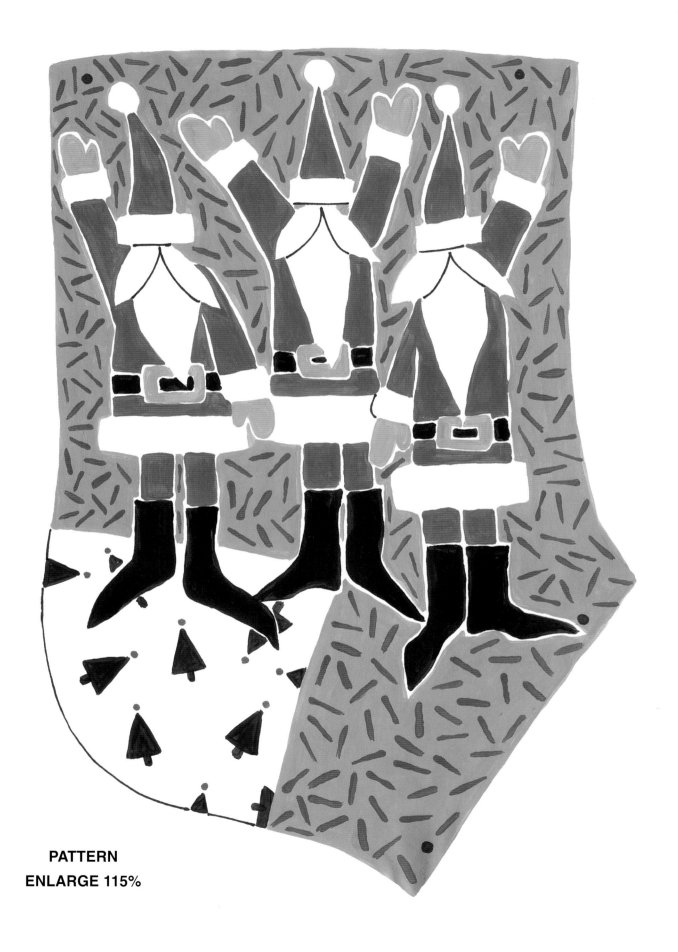

PATTERN
ENLARGE 115%

Angelic
Memories

Angelic Memories

If I had to choose a "favorite" piece created for this book, this would be it. I think the simplicity of the frame, with color on color, worked. This angel frame will probably hang in my dining room.

THINGS YOU'LL NEED:

Wooden frame,
   9¹/₂" square with
   4¹/₂" square opening
Angel, 6" x 12" x ¹/₂" pine
6 Medium stars,
   1" x 6" x ¹/₄" pine
6" x 6" x ¹/₈" balsa wood
   for the following:
   8 Small stars
   4 Large stars
   8 Small hearts
   4 Large hearts
Pencil
Tracing paper
Graphite paper
¹/₂" Flat brush
Small pointed brush
1" Sponge brush
Carving knife or
   heavy-duty X-acto knife

Acrylic paint:
   Butterscotch
   Moon yellow
   Pink
   Turquoise
   White
Oil paint:
   Burnt umber
Mineral spirits
Rag or old cloth
Glue gun and glue sticks
Clear matte spray finish

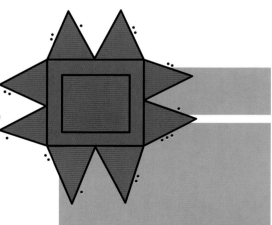

FOLLOW THESE STEPS:

1 Cut the angel and the medium stars from the pine. Cut the stars and the remaining hearts from the ¹/₈" balsa wood. Use the patterns from page 91. Refer to the General Instructions for transferring patterns.

2 Using a carving knife or a heavy-duty X-acto knife, remove small pieces of wood from the edges of the angel so that it appears to have been hand-carved.

3 Using a glue gun, attach the wooden stars and hearts to the frame. Refer to the photograph for suggested placement. Hold in place until secure. Do not use the medium stars.

4 Using a pencil, trace the angel pattern from below onto tracing paper. Using graphite paper, transfer the pattern onto the angel.

5 Using a ¹/₂" flat brush, paint the frame, the hearts, and the stars with moon yellow acrylic paint. Using the ¹/₂" flat brush and the small pointed brush, paint the angel. Paint the dress with turquoise acrylic paint, the hair with butterscotch acrylic paint, and the wing with white acrylic paint. Refer to the pattern. Leave a small amount of space between colors. Leave a space on both sides of the swirls on the wings. Do not paint the swirls. Mix the white and the pink acrylic paints for the face, the hands, and the feet. Leave a space of wood between the hands. Using the small pointed brush, dab a small amount of pink acrylic paint onto the angel's cheek. Using the ¹/₂" flat brush, paint three medium-size stars with moon yellow acrylic paint and three with butterscotch acrylic paint. Let the paint dry between coats.

6 Mix 1 part of burnt umber oil paint to 5 parts of mineral spirits. Using a 1" sponge brush, paint this stain over the front and the sides of the angel. Let the stain dry for about 30 seconds and, using a rag or old cloth, wipe off the remaining stain. Using this stain, paint the medium-size stars and the frame. Let the stain dry for about 45 seconds and, using the rag or old cloth, wipe off the remaining stain.

7 Using the glue gun, attach the angel to the top of the frame. Position her in the center of the frame. Attach the medium stars to the angel's hands. Refer to the photograph for suggested placement.

8 Using clear matte spray finish, spray the frame. Apply a second coat of spray finish to the frame. Let the spray finish dry between coats.

PATTERNS

ENLARGE 130%

To: You
From: Me

Whenever I see crafted pieces with names on them, I always wonder who the names refer to. Ryan is my oldest nephew, now attending the University of Wyoming. Blair is my 9-year-old, love-of-my-life niece. Sara is my best friend's daughter who has always called me "Aunt Linda." Trent is my adorable, athletically talented nephew.

THINGS YOU'LL NEED:

Stockings,
  4" x 5" x ¹⁄₈" balsa wood
  for each stocking
Pencil
Small pointed brush
1" Sponge brush
Fine-grit sandpaper
Clean cloth
Acrylic paint:
  Christmas green
  Christmas red
  Mustard
  White
Oil paint:
  Burnt umber
Mineral spirits
Rag or old cloth
Clear matte spray finish
Double-stick tape or
  drill with ³⁄₁₆" drill bit
  and ribbon or raffia

FOLLOW THESE STEPS:

1 Cut the stockings from the ¹⁄₈" balsa wood. Use the stocking pattern from page 94. Refer to the General Instructions for transferring patterns.

2 Using fine-grit sandpaper, lightly sand the stockings, including the edges, until smooth. Using a clean, damp cloth, wipe the dust from the stocking gift tags. Using a pencil, draw a line across the bottom of the stocking top. Draw the toe and the heel.

Write the name of your choosing in the top of the stocking.

3 Select the design you prefer, from the pattern or from the photograph, and draw it onto the front of the stocking. Using a small pointed brush, paint the name first. Paint each color, leaving a space between colors. Let the paint dry between each color. Dots and small lines are added after the main paint color is applied. Paint around the painted name, the trees, the checks, the hearts and the stars. Paint around the penciled line, marking the heel, the toe, and the stocking top. Refer to the pattern and the photograph for suggested colors for painting.

4 Mix 1 part of burnt umber oil paint to 5 parts of mineral spirits. Using a 1" sponge brush, paint this stain over the stockings. Let the stain dry for about 30 seconds and, using a rag or old cloth, wipe off the remaining stain. The space in between acrylic paint colors will stain darker and act as an outline.

5 Using clear matte spray finish, spray the stockings. Apply a second coat of spray finish to the stockings. Let the spray finish dry between coats.

6 Using double-stick tape, attach the stocking gift tags to your packages, or drill a 3/16" hole in the upper left-hand corner of each stocking and attach them to your packages with a ribbon or raffia.

PATTERN

TYLER

BRET

Idea: New shapes!

94

Dashing
Through
the Snow

Dashing Through the Snow

I didn't include very many holiday projects in this book because I think it is hard to make things to display for just a short time. I did have this little snowman floating around in my head and thought he would be a good addition to the book. When I saw the little wooden sled in a craft store, I knew it was the perfect setting for my little snowman.

THINGS YOU'LL NEED:

Wooden sled
  with rope handle
Wooden star, 1"
Pencil
Tracing paper
Graphite paper
Masking tape
Small pointed brush
1" Sponge brush
Acrylic paint:
  Barnyard red
  Brilliant blue
  Christmas green
  Mustard
  White
  Wrought iron black
Oil paint:
  Burnt umber
Mineral spirits
Rag or old cloth
Glue gun and glue sticks
Clear matte spray finish

FOLLOW THESE STEPS:

1 Using a pencil, trace the snowman and lettering pattern from page 97 onto tracing paper. Using graphite paper, transfer the patterns onto the wooden sled top and runners.

2 Wrap the edges of the rope handle near the wood with masking tape or remove the rope handle until the painting is completed.

3 Using a small pointed brush, paint the snowman

and the snowflakes with white acrylic paint. Paint each color, leaving a space between colors. Paint the star with mustard acrylic paint. Repaint the snowman with white acrylic paint, making sure your brush strokes go in different directions. This will make a difference when you stain your piece. Paint the bottom of the sled and all of the edges with brilliant blue acrylic paint, except under the lettering, which should be painted with white acrylic paint. Also, paint the bottom of the runners with white acrylic paint. Paint the remaining details using the pattern as a guide. Paint the arms, the eyes, and the mouth with wrought iron black acrylic paint. Let the paint dry between coats.

4 Using a glue gun, attach the star to the front center of the wooden sled.

5 Mix 1 part of burnt umber oil paint to 4 parts of mineral spirits. Using a 1" sponge brush, paint this stain over the entire sled. Do not get the stain on the rope handle. Let the stain dry for about 30 sec-onds and, using a rag or old cloth, wipe off the remaining stain. The space in between acrylic paint colors will stain darker and act as an outline. The white snowman and the lettering will be beige in color.

6 Remove the masking tape from the rope handle. Using clear matte spray finish, spray the entire sled. Apply a second coat of spray finish to the sled. Let the spray finish dry between coats. If you removed the rope handle before you began painting, reattach it now.

PATTERNS

Treasures "Deer" to the Heart

This little box was the second piece I created for this book. I just loved the shape of the reindeer and wanted to make something that wouldn't be associated with any particular holiday. I was really proud of myself when I added the little stars, which act as an opening device for the lid. I thought they were the finishing touch for this creation.

THINGS YOU'LL NEED:

Wooden box with
  hinged lid
Wooden deer,
  5" x 7" x 1/8" balsa wood
4" x 6" x 1/8" balsa wood
  for the following:
  3 Medium stars
  7 Small stars
4 Wooden finials,
  approximately 3/4"
  diameter and 1 1/8" high
Medium pointed brush
Fine-grit sandpaper
Clean cloth
Acrylic paint:
  Butter pecan
  Light gray

Fine-point permanent
  gold marker
Glue gun and glue sticks
  or Tacky glue
Textured rag or cheese cloth
Paper towels
Clear matte spray finish

FOLLOW THESE STEPS:

1 Cut the deer and the stars from the 1/8" balsa wood. Use the patterns from page 100. Refer to the General Instructions for transferring patterns.

2 Using fine-grit sandpaper, lightly sand the deer and the stars. Using a clean, damp cloth, wipe the dust from the deer and stars.

3 Using a glue gun or Tacky glue, glue the wooden finials to the bottom four corners of the wooden box to create legs. Hold in place until secure.

4 Using a medium pointed brush, paint the inside and the outside of the wooden box and its legs with butter pecan acrylic paint. Paint both sides and the

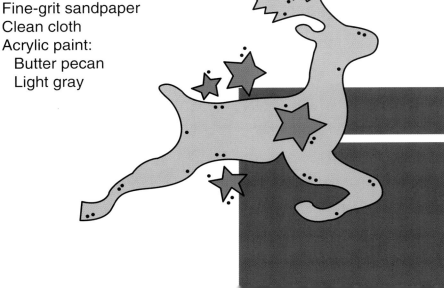

edges of the deer with butter pecan acrylic paint. Let the paint dry between coats.

5 Using a textured rag or cheese cloth, dip into light gray acrylic paint. Press the rag onto a paper towel. Gently dab the paint onto the wooden box. Repeat this process until the wooden box and legs are covered. Make sure much of the butter pecan coloring still shows through the "dabs." Repeat this process on both sides of the deer. Refer to the General Instructions for spackling and texturing techniques. Do not "texture" the inside of the box. Let the paint dry between coats.

6 Using a fine-point permanent gold marker, color the fronts and sides of all the stars. Let the marker dry.

7 Using the glue gun or Tacky glue, attach the three medium stars together. Position the stars on the lid and glue them into place to create a handle. Glue three small stars on each side of the deer according to the pattern. Attach the deer to the top of the wooden box, centering it in the middle. Refer to the photograph for suggested placement.

8 Using clear matte spray finish, spray the inside of the wooden box. Let the spray finish dry. Close the lid and spray the entire outside of the box. Apply a second coat of spray finish to the outside of the box. Let the spray finish dry between coats.

Idea: If your home needs a color boost, try a different paint combination

PATTERNS

SELECT TWO STAR SIZES TO USE ON YOUR BOX!

Simple
But
Shapely

Simple But Shapely

I had all of these little wooden finials and spools which were really crafted for other purposes. They were in a bucket by my desk for a long, long time. Finally I picked them up and started inserting one piece into another and gluing them together. Because they are lightweight, I thought they would make ideal Christmas tree ornaments.

THINGS YOU'LL NEED:

Variety of wooden finials,
  with at least one flat edge
Variety of wooden wheels
Variety of wooden plugs
1/2" Flat brush
Acrylic paint:
  Metallic gold
  White
Fine-point permanent
  gold marker
Glue gun and glue sticks
Metallic gold spray
Newspaper
Embellishments,
  your choice

FOLLOW THESE STEPS:

1 Using a glue gun, attach the finials, the wheels, and/or the plugs to create an ornament. Make sure it isn't too heavy to hang on a tree branch.

2 Using a 1/2" flat brush, paint alternating areas of each ornament with white acrylic paint. Apply a second coat of white acrylic paint to the ornaments. Let the paint dry between coats. Paint the remaining areas of each ornament with metallic gold acrylic paint. Let the paint dry.

3 Using a fine-point permanent gold marker, draw the design of your choice onto the white areas of each ornament. Refer to Diagram A. Let the marker dry.

4 Lay the painted ornaments on newspaper. Using metallic gold spray, spray one side of each ornament. Let the metallic spray dry. Turn the ornaments over to spray the other side. Let the metallic spray dry between coats. Embellish as desired.

DIAGRAM A

On the
Wings
of Angels

On the Wings of Angels

I designed the wings and body, had them cut, then I painted and adorned them. Her coloring was inspired by my two oldest nieces, Nichole and Ashley. My nephew, Matthew, is also a blondie, but I'm not sure any of my nieces or nephews are angels!

THINGS YOU'LL NEED:

Angel,
  5" x 11" x $^1/_8$" balsa wood
Wings,
  $4^1/_2$" x 14" x $^1/_8$" balsa wood
4 Medium stars
4 Small stars
2 Tiny stars
3 Hearts
6 Variegated
  brown / beige buttons, $^1/_4$"
Pencil
$^1/_4$" Flat brush
Small pointed brush
1" Sponge brush
Carving knife or
  heavy-duty X-acto knife

Acrylic paint:
  Linen beige
  Metallic gold
  Moon yellow
  Pink
  White
Oil paint:
  Burnt umber
Mineral spirits
Rag or old cloth
Fine-point permanent
  black marker
Glue gun and glue sticks
  or Tacky glue
Clear matte spray finish

FOLLOW THESE STEPS:

1 Cut the angel and the wings from the $^1/_8$" balsa wood. Use the patterns from pages 105 and 106. Refer to the General Instructions for transferring patterns.

2 Using a carving knife or a heavy-duty X-acto knife, remove small pieces of wood from the edges of the angel and the wings so they appear to have been hand-carved.

3 Using a pencil, trace the pattern on the front and back of the angel's body onto tracing paper. Using graphite paper, transfer the pattern onto the wood. Refer to the pattern.

4 Using a $^1/_4$" flat brush, paint the three hearts with metallic gold acrylic paint. Paint one medium star and the wings with metallic

gold acrylic paint. Paint all the remaining stars and the shoes with linen beige acrylic paint. Paint the bodice and the sleeves of the dress with linen beige acrylic paint. Paint the bottom of the dress and the collar of the dress with white acrylic paint. Using the small pointed brush, paint the angel's hair with moon yellow acrylic paint. Mix a small amount of pink acrylic paint with white acrylic paint and paint the angel's face, hands, and legs. Lightly brush the cheeks with pink acrylic paint. When painting, leave the pencil or traced line un-painted so the wood is ex-posed. When the figure is stained, the stain will remain in the unpainted areas and create an outline. Paint the back of the angel. Use the same pattern to paint the legs, hands, and shoes as used on the front of the an-gel. Let the paint dry between coats.

5 Mix 1 part of burnt umber oil paint to 4 parts of min-eral spirits. Using a 1" sponge brush, paint this stain over the front of the angel. Let the stain dry for about 20 seconds and, using a rag or old cloth, wipe off the remain-ing stain. Repeat this process on the back side of the angel and on all the hearts, the stars, and the wings. Using this stain, brush on all edges and allow the stain to dry full strength. Do not apply as much mixture to the face, the hands, or the legs.

6 Using a glue gun or Tacky glue, attach the wings to the back of the angel's body. Refer to the photograph for placement. Attach the hearts, the stars, and the buttons. Refer to the photograph for suggested placement.

7 Using a fine-point perma-nent black marker, draw the closed eyelids above the cheeks on the face. Draw vertical lines between the but-tons. Refer to the pattern for suggested placement.

8 Using clear matte spray finish, spray the angel and wings. Apply a second coat of spray finish to the an-gel and wings. Let the spray finish dry between coats.

PATTERNS

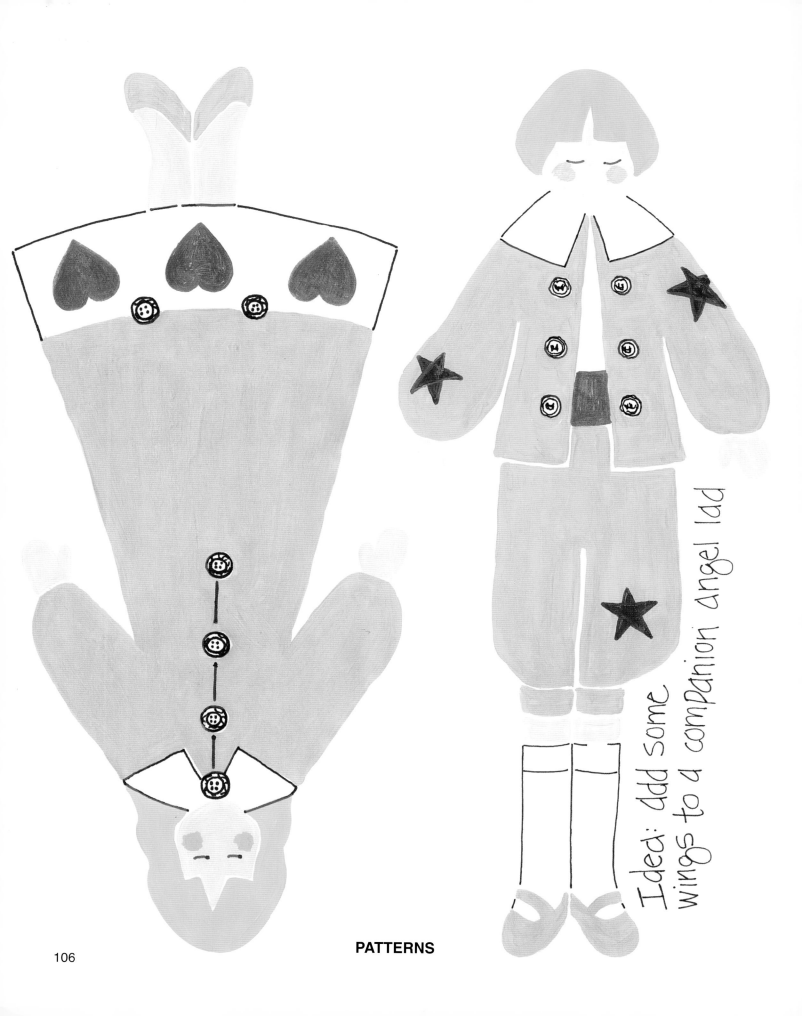

Idea: add some wings to a companion Angel lad

PATTERNS

South of the
Border

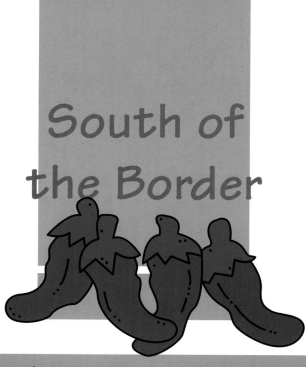

South of the Border

That Southwestern influence keeps creeping into my designs. I have about eight of these stockings hanging from drawer pulls on a huge shelf in my dining room each Christmas. I thought I would add just a touch of decoration and make the stocking something that would work as a wall accessory in a kitchen all year long.

THINGS YOU'LL NEED:

4 Chiles,
  8" x 4" x $\frac{1}{8}$" balsa wood
Tan suede, $\frac{1}{2}$ yard
Fleece, $1\frac{1}{4}$" x 9"
Pencil
Tracing paper
Graphite paper
Small pointed brush
Carving knife or
  heavy-duty X-acto knife
Fine-grit sandpaper
Clean cloth
Acrylic paint:
  Barnyard red
  Plantation green
Matching thread
Tacky glue
Clear matte spray finish

FOLLOW THESE STEPS:

For the Chiles:

1 Cut the chiles from the $\frac{1}{8}$" balsa wood. Use the chile pattern from page 109. Refer to the General Instructions for transferring patterns.

2 Using a carving knife or a heavy-duty X-acto knife, remove small pieces of wood from the edges of the chiles so they appear to have been hand-carved.

3 Using fine-grit sandpaper, lightly sand the chiles.

Using a clean, damp cloth, wipe the dust from the chiles.

4 Using a pencil, draw the chile tops on one side of the chiles. Refer to the pattern.

5 Using a small pointed brush, paint the tops and sides of the chiles with plantation green acrylic paint. Paint the chiles on the front and sides with barnyard red acrylic paint. Let the paint dry between coats.

6 Lay the chiles on a clean, flat surface. Using clear matte spray finish, spray the chiles. Let the spray finish dry. Turn the chiles over and spray. Let the spray finish dry. Apply a second coat of spray finish to both sides of the chiles. Let the spray finish dry between coats.

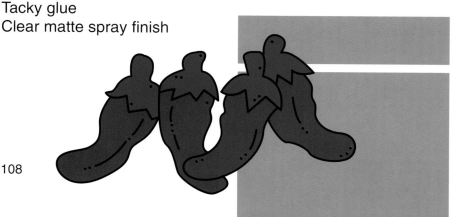

For the Stocking:

1 Using the pencil, trace the stocking pattern below onto tracing paper. Add 2¹/₂" to the top of the stocking and add ¹/₈" around the entire pattern, except for the top edge, for a seam. Using graphite paper, transfer the pattern onto the suede twice. Cut two stockings— each going in the opposite direction to allow seams to align. Cut one 6" x ¹/₂" wide strip of suede for the hanger.

2 Place the suede stocking pieces, right sides together, and sew, using a ¹/₈" seam allowance with matching thread. Do not sew the stocking across the top.

3 Turn the stocking right side out. Fold the 6" strip in half lengthwise. Attach it to the outside edge of the stocking on the heel side, opposite the toe end, using Tacky glue. Glue the fleece to the top edge over the hanger attachment, starting at the seam. Overlap fleece on fleece and glue in place. The top edge of the fleece should line up with the top edge of the suede.

4 Using Tacky glue, attach the chiles to the suede just below the fleece. Place the Tacky glue behind the "green" part of the chiles so the chiles will appear to be hanging.

NOTE: Be sure to add 2¹/₂" to the top of the stocking before cutting the pattern.

Idea: Hang a new wooden figure on the stocking

PATTERN

STOCKING PATTERN

Once Upon a Tiny Forest

The little reindeer on top of this frame was so adorable I couldn't resist putting him into a piece. I purchased the frame at a local import store. It was a horrible color and it tickled me to repaint and redecorate it. I worked at keeping the frame simple so that it would not compete with the photograph that would go into it.

THINGS YOU'LL NEED:

Wooden frame,
  6$^1/_2$" x 8" x $^3/_4$" with
  3$^1/_2$" x 5" opening
2" x 6" x $^1/_2$" pine
  for the following:
    4 Wooden pine trees
    Wooden reindeer
Ruler
Pencil
$^1/_2$" Flat brush
Small pointed brush
Acrylic paint:
  Brilliant blue
  Calico red
  Plantation green
  Wicker white
Old toothbrush
Glue gun and glue sticks
  or Tacky glue
Clear matte spray finish

FOLLOW THESE STEPS:

1 Cut the trees and the reindeer from the $^1/_2$" pine. Use the patterns from page 112. Refer to the General Instructions for transferring patterns.

2 Remove the backing and the glass from the frame. Using a ruler and a pencil, draw a $^3/_8$" line around the inside edge of the frame—the edge which will border the photograph or picture.

3 Using a small pointed brush, paint the inside $^3/_8$"

area around the opening and the sides of the frame where it will meet the glass with brilliant blue acrylic paint. Using a $^1/_2$" flat brush, paint the remainder of the front and the sides of the frame with calico red acrylic paint. Paint all the trees with plantation green acrylic paint, making sure to paint the front, back, and all sides of each piece. You may have to apply a second coat for full coverage. Let the paint dry between coats. Paint the reindeer with brilliant blue acrylic paint, making sure to paint the front, back, and all sides. You may have to apply a second coat for full coverage. Let the paint dry between coats.

4 Using a glue gun or Tacky glue, attach the trees and the reindeer to the top of the frame. Hold in place until secure. Refer to the photograph for suggested placement.

5 Dip an old toothbrush into wicker white acrylic paint. Using your finger, "flip" the paint onto the front and the sides of the frame from a distance of about six inches. Using this technique, paint the trees and the reindeer. Refer to the General Instructions for painting with a toothbrush. Let the paint dry.

6 Using clear matte spray finish, spray the frame. Let the spray finish dry. Apply a second coat of spray finish to the frame. Let the spray finish dry.

7 Place the glass, a photograph or picture, and the backing on the frame.

PATTERNS

southwest frame toppers

more Ideas

holiday bunnies or decor for baby's room

an apple for the teacher

Home Tweet Home

Home Tweet Home

I love birdhouses and I couldn't stop with just one. The shelf stimulated a family night when all of my nieces and nephews painted birdhouses, too. Matthew, Ashley, Blair, Trent, Jordan, and Chase now have marvelous treasures they made for themselves!

THINGS YOU'LL NEED:

Wooden shelf,
 5¹/₂" high x 13" long x
 5¹/₂" deep
3 Wooden birdhouses with
 4"-wide x 4¹/₂"-deep bases
Cow,
 3" x 3" x ¹/₂" pine
12" x 4" x ¹/₈" balsa wood
 for the following:
 11 Medium stars
 2 Moons
¹/₂"-Square stencil
1" Star stencil
2³/₄" Star stencil
Ruler
Pencil
Tracing paper
Graphite paper
¹/₂" Flat brush
Small pointed brush
Stencil brush
Spackling knife
Spackling compound

Fine-grit sandpaper
Clean cloth
Flat black spray paint
Acrylic paint:
 Barnyard red
 Brilliant blue
 Buttercrunch
 Slate blue
 Teddy bear tan
 Thicket green
 White
 Wicker white
 Wrought iron black
Medium-point permanent
 black marker
Old toothbrush
Glue gun and glue sticks
Clear matte spray finish

FOLLOW THESE STEPS:

1 Cut the cow from the ¹/₂" pine and the stars and the moons from the ¹/₈" balsa wood. Use the patterns from page 116. Refer to the General Instructions for transferring patterns.

2 Using a spackling knife, spackle the staple holes in the wood with spackling compound. Refer to the General Instructions for spackling and texturing techniques. Let the spackling compound dry completely.

3 Using a ¹/₂" flat brush, paint the cow with white acrylic paint on both sides and on all edges. Paint one side and the edges of the moons with teddy bear tan acrylic paint. Paint one side and the edges of five stars with buttercrunch acrylic paint. Paint one side and the edges of three stars with barnyard red acrylic paint. Paint one side and the edges of the remaining three stars with white acrylic paint. Let the paint dry between coats.

4 Using fine-grit sandpaper, lightly sand the cow, the moons, and the stars. Using a clean, damp cloth, wipe the dust from the cow, moons, and stars.

5 Using a medium-point permanent black marker, draw irregular circles on both sides of the cow and color them with the marker. Refer to the pattern for suggested placement.

6 Remove all the perches from the birdhouses before you begin painting. Paint one perch with thicket green acrylic paint and one with tan acrylic paint. You will not use the third perch, but you may want to keep it in case you should need to replace one of the others.

7 **Birdhouse 1 (Barn):** Using the 1/2" flat brush, paint the walls, the base of the barn, and the inside edge of the birdhouse opening with barnyard red acrylic paint. Paint the roof and the eaves with wrought iron black acrylic paint, except for the top left side (as it faces you). Paint the remaining roof panel with wicker white acrylic paint. Using a ruler and a pencil, draw five lines, spaced equally apart, on the wicker white colored roof. This will create six stripes. In the back top corner, draw a box which is 2 1/4" long by 2 drawn lines high. Using the 1" star stencil, draw two stars in the box. Refer to Diagram A. Using a small pointed brush, paint alternating stripes, starting with the top stripe, with barnyard red acrylic paint. Paint the area around the stenciled stars with brilliant blue acrylic paint. Center the 2 3/4" star stencil over the round opening in the birdhouse. Using a stencil brush, stencil with brilliant blue acrylic paint. Let the paint dry. Using fine-grit sandpaper, lightly sand all the edges of the roof, the barn, and the base. Using a glue gun, attach the cow's rear end to the front of the barn where the perch was located. Hold in place until secure. Set aside.

Birdhouse 2: Using the 1/2" flat brush, paint the walls, the base of the house, and the inside edge of the birdhouse opening with thicket green acrylic paint. Paint the roof and the eaves with buttercrunch acrylic paint. Place the 2 3/4" star stencil over the round opening in the birdhouse. Using the stencil brush, stencil with barnyard red acrylic paint. Using the 1/2" square stencil, center over one side of the roof. If the squares are not complete, the unfinished square should be at the top of the roof. Stencil with thicket green acrylic paint over the buttercrunch acrylic paint. Repeat on the other side of the roof. Using fine-grit sandpaper, lightly sand the edges of the roof, the house, the perch, and the three barnyard red colored stars. Using a glue gun, attach two stars to the right side of the birdhouse roof and one star on the left side. Refer to Diagram B. Set aside.

Birdhouse 3: Using the 1/2" flat brush, paint the walls, the base of the house, and the inside edge of the birdhouse opening with teddy bear tan acrylic paint. Paint the roof and the eaves with slate blue acrylic paint. Dip an old toothbrush into the tan acrylic paint. Using your finger, "flip" the paint onto the roof and the eaves of the house. Don't worry if the paint gets on the house—it is the same color. Refer to the General Instructions for painting with a toothbrush. Place the 2 3/4" star stencil over the round opening in the birdhouse. Using the stencil brush, stencil with buttercrunch acrylic paint. Using the pencil, draw small triangles around the birdhouse opening. Don't worry if they are not perfectly even. They should be about 3/8" high from the opening. Using the small pointed brush, paint the triangles with buttercrunch acrylic paint. Refer to the photograph. Using fine-grit sandpaper, lightly sand the edges of the roof, the eaves, the house, the base, and the perch. Using a glue gun, attach three stars to the right side of the roof and two stars and a moon to the left side of the roof. Refer to Diagram B. Set aside.

8 Using flat black spray paint, spray the shelf. Let the spray paint dry completely. Using fine-grit sandpaper, lightly sand the edges of the shelf. Using the clean, damp cloth, wipe the dust from the shelf. Using the pencil, trace the lettering pattern from below onto tracing paper. Using graphite paper, transfer the lettering to the shelf. Using the small pointed brush, paint the lettering with buttercrunch acrylic paint. Don't worry about the lines having irregular thicknesses —this will enhance the project. Dip an old toothbrush into buttercrunch acrylic paint. Using your finger, "flip" the mixture onto the shelf from a distance of about six inches. Using this technique, paint the shelf on all sides. Refer to the General Instructions for painting with a toothbrush. Let the paint dry. Using a glue gun, attach the remaining three white colored stars and the moon to the shelf. Refer to the photograph for suggested placement. Attach the three birdhouses to the top of the shelf. The birdhouses should be placed on the shelf so that they do not interfere with the shelf being hung tightly against the wall. Glue the perches to the appropriate birdhouses.

9 Using a clear matte spray finish, spray the birdhouses and the shelf. Apply two additional coats of spray finish to the birdhouses and shelf. Let the spray finish dry between coats.

DIAGRAM A

DIAGRAM B

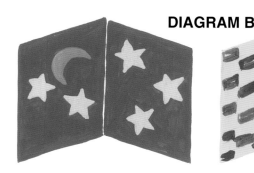 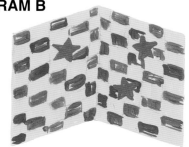

PATTERNS

Tweet Tweet Time to sleep

How Does
Your
Garden Grow?

Your Garden Grow?

How Does

I have always been an avid outdoors person and especially like the mountains. One day, my friend Jo and I were shopping and she bought a set of unique garden tools to use when photographing projects for her books. This stimulated me to combine the tree with the harvesting theme and create this rack for garden tools.

THINGS YOU'LL NEED:

8¹/₂" x 18" x ³/₄" pine
4" x 12" x ¹/₈" balsa wood
  for the following:
   3 Wooden hearts
   4 Wooden birds
Pencil
Tracing paper
Graphite paper
¹/₂" Flat brush
Small pointed brush
1" Sponge brush
Carving knife or
  heavy-duty X-acto knife
Fine-grit sandpaper
Clean cloth
Acrylic paint:
  Barnyard red
  Brilliant blue
  Buttercrunch
  Tangerine
  Thicket green
  Wicker white

Oil paint:
  Burnt umber
Mineral spirits
Rag or old cloth
Fine-point permanent
  black marker
Glue gun and glue sticks
Clear matte spray finish
3 Wardrobe hooks,
  antique brass
Screwdriver

FOLLOW THESE STEPS:

1 Cut the rack from the ³/₄" pine and the hearts and the birds from the ¹/₈" balsa wood. Use the patterns from page 120. Refer to the General Instructions for transferring patterns.

2 Using a carving knife or a heavy-duty X-acto knife, remove small pieces of wood from the front and back edges of the trees so they appear to have been hand-carved. Repeat the process on one side of the edges of the hearts. Do not carve the birds.

3 Using a pencil, trace the patterns for the words from page 119 onto tracing paper. Using graphite paper, transfer the words onto the hearts.

4 Using a ½" flat brush, paint the front and all the edges of the rack with thicket green acrylic paint. Use only one coat—don't worry about leaving brush strokes. Paint the carved side and all the edges of the hearts with barnyard red acrylic paint. Leave an unpainted edge around all the lettering on the hearts. Using a small pointed brush, paint *around* the lettering on the hearts. Let the paint dry between coats. Refer to Diagram A. Using the ½" flat brush, paint both sides and all of the edges of one bird with buttercrunch acrylic paint, both sides and all of the edges of one bird with brilliant blue acrylic paint, and both sides and all of the edges of two birds with wicker white acrylic paint. Paint the birds' beaks with tangerine acrylic paint. Let the paint dry between coats.

5 Using fine-grit sandpaper, lightly sand the edges of the rack, the hearts, and the birds. Using a clean, damp cloth, wipe the dust from the rack, hearts, and birds.

6 Using a glue gun, attach one heart to the center of each tree. From left to right, the words should read: "Plant, Sow, Reap." Refer to the photograph for suggested placement. Attach the birds. Refer to the photograph for suggested placement.

7 Mix 1 part of burnt umber oil paint to 4 parts of mineral spirits. Using a 1" sponge brush, paint this stain over the front of the rack. Let the stain dry for about 30 seconds and, using a rag or old cloth, wipe off the remaining stain. Repeat this process on the hearts and the birds. After this process on the hearts, the lettering will appear wider.

8 Using a fine-point permanent black marker, dot an eye on each bird. Draw a line on the body of each bird to create the appearance of a wing. Refer to the pattern for suggested placement. Draw small leaves around the words on the hearts. Refer to the pattern for suggested placement.

9 Using clear matte spray finish, spray the rack. Apply a second coat of spray finish to the rack. Let the spray finish dry between coats. Using a screwdriver, attach one wardrobe hook to the center bottom of each tree on the tree base.

DIAGRAM A

Idea: Try a different phrase

LIVE
LOVE
LAUGH

It's
the
Journey

Plant
Sow
Reap

PATTERNS

120

Everybody
Loves a
Parade

Everybody Loves a Parade

Gardens remind me of parades! The cabbages are all in a row next to the zucchini plants and tomatoes, systematically aligned. Corn usually takes up two rows, but each vegetable produces a different shape, color, and texture—just like a parade. The birds on this garden marker can hear John Philip Sussa, don't you think?

THINGS YOU'LL NEED:

9" x 3" x $^3/_4$" pine with
  arch on center top
4" x 8" x $^1/_8$" balsa wood
  for the following:
  6 Wooden birds
  Wooden heart
Wooden dowel, 14" x $^1/_8$"
Wood glue
Drill with $^1/_8$" drill bit
Pencil
Tracing paper
Graphite paper
$^1/_2$" Flat brush
Small pointed brush
1" Sponge brush

Acrylic paint:
  Barnyard red
  Buttercrunch
  Purple
  Tangerine
  Turquoise
  White
  Wrought iron black
Oil paint:
  Burnt umber
Mineral spirits
Rag or old cloth
Fine-point permanent
  black marker
Glue gun and glue sticks
Clear matte spray finish

FOLLOW THESE STEPS:

1 Cut the garden marker from the $^3/_4$" pine and the birds and the hearts from the $^1/_8$" balsa wood. Use the patterns from page 124. Refer to the General Instructions for transferring patterns.

2 Using a drill with a $^1/_8$" drill bit, drill a 1"-deep hole in the bottom of the garden marker. Using wood glue, glue the wooden dowel into the hole.

3 Using a pencil, trace the garden marker pattern from page 124 onto tracing paper. Using graphite paper, transfer the pattern onto one side of the garden marker. Trace the heart pattern from page 124 onto tracing paper. Using graphite paper, transfer the pattern onto one side of the heart.

4 Using a ¹/₂" flat brush, paint the side of the garden marker that does not have the pattern on it with turquoise acrylic paint. On the patterned side of the garden marker, paint the background with buttercrunch acrylic paint. Let the paint dry between coats. Leave an unpainted edge around all the lettering. Using a small pointed brush, paint *around* the lettering. Use only one coat—you don't need to have full coverage.

5 Using the pencil, draw a line down the center on all sides of the garden marker. Don't worry if the lines are not perfectly even. Divide the garden marker into ¹/₂"-wide squares. Don't worry if the squares are not perfect. Refer to Diagram A.

6 Using the ¹/₂" flat brush, paint alternating squares with turquoise acrylic paint. Paint the remaining squares with purple acrylic paint. Leave the pencil lines exposed between the squares. The turquoise colored squares should not touch the purple colored squares. Refer to Diagram A. Paint both sides and all of the edges of one bird with white acrylic paint, both sides and all of the edges of one bird with purple acrylic paint, both sides and all of the edges of one bird with turquoise acrylic paint, both sides and all of

the edges of one bird with barnyard red acrylic paint, both sides and all of the edges of one bird with buttercrunch acrylic paint, and both sides and all of the edges of one bird with wrought iron black acrylic paint. Paint the birds' beaks with tangerine acrylic paint. All the birds' beaks should be facing left as you look at them, except for the turquoise colored bird. Refer to the photograph for suggested placement. Using the small pointed brush, paint the word "loves" on the heart with purple acrylic paint. Paint the remaining words on the garden marker with purple acrylic paint. Leave a thick line of unpainted wood between the purple lettering and the buttercrunch colored background. On the heart, paint the squares between the graphite lines with barnyard red acrylic paint. Leave a space around the words— don't let the barnyard red acrylic paint touch the purple acrylic paint. Extend the pattern to the sides of the heart. Refer to the pattern. Paint the back side of the heart solid with barnyard red acrylic paint. Let the paint dry between coats.

7 Mix 1 part of burnt umber oil paint to 5 parts of mineral spirits. Using a 1" sponge brush, paint this stain over the front of the garden marker. Let the stain dry for about 30 seconds and, using a rag or old cloth, wipe off the remaining stain. Repeat this process on the back of the garden marker, the sides of the garden marker, the dowel, and the fronts and the sides of the heart and the birds.

8 Using a fine-point permanent black marker, dot an eye on each bird.

9 Using a glue gun, attach the heart to the garden marker. It should be tilted slightly from the left to the right. Refer to the pattern for suggested placement. Attach the birds to the garden marker and the heart. Refer to the photograph for suggested placement.

10 Using clear matte spray finish, spray the back side of the garden marker. Spray the front side of the garden marker. Apply five additional coats of spray finish to the front side of the garden marker. Let the spray finish dry between coats.

DIAGRAM A

PATTERNS

Everybody Loves a Parade

Idea: a marker for your vegetable garden

I CAN'T WAIT TO EAT!

Celestial
Fantasy

Celestial Fantasy

I made this plate for my friend Beverly White. She was sitting at the table watching me paint and said she wanted the plate when I was through using it for the book. Gladly, I agreed. It was flattering to know someone liked my work. We were on a golf vacation, but as the book deadline drew nearer, I had to create wooden projects wherever we went!

THINGS YOU'LL NEED:

12½" wooden plate
  with a decorative rim and
  8" center section
Ruler
Pencil
½" Flat brush
Acrylic paint:
  Metallic gold
  Navy blue
Medium-point permanent
  gold marker
Clear matte spray finish

FOLLOW THESE STEPS:

1 Using a ½" flat brush, paint the entire top side of the wooden plate with navy blue acrylic paint. Paint the inside section of the back side of the wooden plate with navy blue acrylic paint. Paint the outside rim on the back of the wooden plate with metallic gold acrylic paint. Apply additional coats of acrylic paint until full coverage on the plate is achieved. Let the paint dry between coats.

2 Using a pencil, draw a 3¼" circle in the middle of the plate. Starting at the outside of the circle, draw a line in a circular motion until you reach the center of the plate. This will create the center of the sun. Refer to the photograph. From the outside of the circle, using a ruler, measure nine 1" lines around the edges of the 3¼" circle. Leave about ¼" between the circle and the lines you will draw. From the end of each 1" mark, draw a diagonal line to the outside edge of the navy blue area so the lines meet to form a triangle. These are the sun's rays. Refer to the photograph. Using a medium-point permanent gold marker, draw an irregular line to outline the triangles you just created. Fill

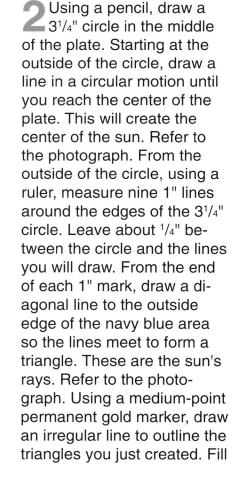

the triangles, leaving some of the navy blue exposed through the permanent gold marker. Refer to the photograph. Draw an irregular line over the circular line in the center of the sun. Expand the line so that only about 1/4" of navy blue shows between the circular lines. Leave some of the navy blue exposed through the permanent gold marker.

3 Using the pencil, draw four moons on the rim of the plate. Draw stars of differ-ent sizes between the moons. Don't worry about the moons and stars being irregular in shape and size. Using the permanent gold marker, fill in the moons, leaving some of the navy blue exposed through the permanent gold marker. Completely fill in the stars. Make dots around the moons and the stars on the rim of the plate. Refer to the photograph for suggested placement.

4 Using the permanent gold marker, paint the inside decorative trim between the outside rim of the plate and the center of the plate. Paint the outside edge of the plate. Let the marker dry.

5 Using clear matte spray finish, spray the back side of the plate. Let the spray finish dry. Spray the front side of the plate. Apply additional coats of spray finish to the front of the plate if the plate will be used to serve food.

Idea: try a different design

moon, sailboat or design

on the center of the plate

Where's the Goose That Laid These Golden Eggs?

I think this is one of my favorites. The colors are rich and, because they are different from typically pastel Easter eggs, I leave my dozen displayed in my dining room year-round. I get a kick out of visitors who are so inclined to lift an egg and even tap it on the edge of my table. Some day I'll add a few real eggs and really get an unexpected reaction!

THINGS YOU'LL NEED:

12 Wooden eggs,
   approximately 2$^1\!/_2$" long x
   2" wide at the center
12-cup egg carton
$^1\!/_2$" Flat brush
Fine-grit sandpaper
Clean cloth
Acrylic paint:
   Metallic gold
   Navy blue
   Wicker white
Old toothbrush
Fine-point permanent
   gold marker
Textured cloth
Clear matte spray finish
Newspaper
Paper towels
Raffia

FOLLOW THESE STEPS:

1 Using fine-grit sandpaper, lightly sand all the wooden eggs. Using a clean, damp cloth, wipe the dust from the eggs.

2 Using a $^1\!/_2$" flat brush, paint four wooden eggs with navy blue acrylic paint, four wooden eggs with wicker white acrylic paint, and four wooden eggs with metallic gold acrylic paint. Apply three coats of acrylic paint to each egg. Let the paint dry completely between coats.

3 One of the metallic gold colored eggs should be left solid gold. The three remaining metallic gold colored eggs should be painted with wicker white acrylic paint, by dipping an old toothbrush into the wicker white acrylic paint. Using your finger, "flip" the acrylic paint onto all sides of the eggs from a distance of about six inches. Refer to the General Instructions for painting with a toothbrush. Let the paint dry.

4 Using a fine-point permanent gold marker, paint one of the wicker white colored eggs and one of the navy blue colored eggs with each of the designs in Diagram A.

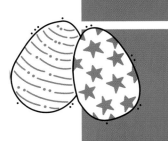

5 On the remaining wicker white colored eggs and the remaining navy blue colored eggs, dip a textured cloth into a small amount of metallic gold acrylic paint, and, after patting the cloth almost dry onto paper towels, "pat" the paint onto the eggs. Refer to the General Instructions for rag painting techniques.

6 Place the painted wooden eggs on newspaper. Using clear matte spray finish, spray the eggs. Let the spray finish dry. Turn the eggs over and spray again. Apply a second coat of spray finish to the eggs. Let the spray finish dry between coats.

7 Place a small amount of raffia into the bottom of each "egg cup" in the egg carton and place the painted eggs into the egg carton.

DIAGRAM A

Idea: More patterns and color combos

130

may the spirit of Christmas live in your heart all year long

All Season Santa

All Season Santa

I have many Santas and I almost cry when I have to box them up and put them in the basement after Christmas. I created this piece to have some year-round appeal. Maybe this Santa won't have to see the inside of a storage box. Maybe he'll be able to see flowers bloom and grass grow—Florida Santas have that luxury, Utah Santas don't.

THINGS YOU'LL NEED:

5" x 7" pine base
  with sculpted edges
12" x 6" x ¹/₂" pine
Wooden heart,
  10" x 6" x ¹/₂" pine
Wooden tree, 3" tall x ¹/₂" pine
2 Wooden houses, 3" tall,
  three-dimensional
  miniatures
Carving knife or
  heavy-duty X-acto knife
Pencil
Tracing paper
Graphite paper
¹/₂" Flat brush
1" Sponge brush

Acrylic paint:
  Acorn brown
  Barnyard red
  Black
  Buttercrunch
  Dark green
  White
Oil paint:
  Burnt umber
Mineral spirits
Rag or old cloth
Fine-point permanent
  gold marker
Glue gun and glue sticks
Clear matte spray finish

FOLLOW THESE STEPS:

1 Cut the Santa and the heart from the ¹/₂" pine. Use the patterns from page 134 and 135. Refer to the General Instructions for transferring patterns.

2 Using a carving knife or a heavy-duty X-acto knife, remove small pieces of wood from the edges of the Santa, the heart, the houses, and the wooden base so they appear to have been hand-carved.

3 Using a ¹/₂" flat brush, paint both sides and the edges of the heart with barnyard red acrylic paint. Using a pencil, draw an irregular, undulating line around the bottom edge of the wooden base. Using the ¹/₂" flat brush, paint the bottom part

with black acrylic paint. Paint the upper part and the top of the wooden base with white acrylic paint. Draw a snow line on the top of the tree. Refer to the photograph for suggested placement. Paint both sides and edges of the tree with dark green acrylic paint and the top of the tree with white acrylic paint. Let the paint dry between coats.

4 Draw an irregular line on the roofs of the houses. Paint the bottom part of the roofs with black acrylic paint. Paint the top part of the roofs with white acrylic paint so they appear to have snow on them. Draw a window and a door on one side of each of the houses. Draw a triangular roof line above the door with snow on top of the triangles. Paint the triangles with black acrylic paint. Paint the snow with white acrylic paint. Paint the rest of the houses with buttercrunch acrylic paint. Paint the doors and the windows with acorn brown acrylic paint. Leave the pencil lines free from any paint. Paint the top edges of the heart with white acrylic paint. Let the paint dry between coats.

5 Using the pencil, trace the Santa pattern from page 134 onto tracing paper. Using graphite paper, transfer the pattern onto both sides of the Santa. Using the small pointed brush, paint the Santa on both sides and on the edges. Refer to the pattern for suggested colors for

painting. Leave the pencil lines free from any paint—do not touch the barnyard red acrylic paint to the white acrylic paint or the black acrylic paint. Let the paint dry between coats.

6 Mix 1 part of burnt umber oil paint to 8 parts of mineral spirits. Using a 1" sponge brush, paint this stain over both sides of the Santa. Let the stain dry for about 30 seconds and, using a rag or old cloth, wipe off the remaining stain. Repeat this process on both sides of the heart, the wooden base, the tree, and the houses. Let the stain dry completely.

7 Using the pencil, trace the lettering pattern from page 135 onto tracing paper. Using graphite paper, transfer the lettering onto both sides of the heart. Using the fine-point permanent gold marker, trace over the transferred lettering. Draw window panes on the windows of the houses and make a doorknob.

8 Using a glue gun, attach the heart to the wooden base on a diagonal from corner to corner. Attach one of the houses to the wooden base on one side, making sure the lettering on the heart is not covered. Attach the tree and another house to the other side of the wooden base, making sure the lettering on the heart is not covered. Balance the Santa on the heart and, using the glue gun, attach it. The Santa

should be placed almost parallel to the front edge of the wooden base when balanced on the heart. Refer to the photograph for suggested placement.

9 Using clear matte spray finish, spray the Santa, the heart, and the base on both sides. Apply a second coat of spray finish to the Santa, heart, and base. Let the spray finish dry between coats. Don't spray the spray finish too close to the permanent gold marker, as it might run.

PATTERN

134

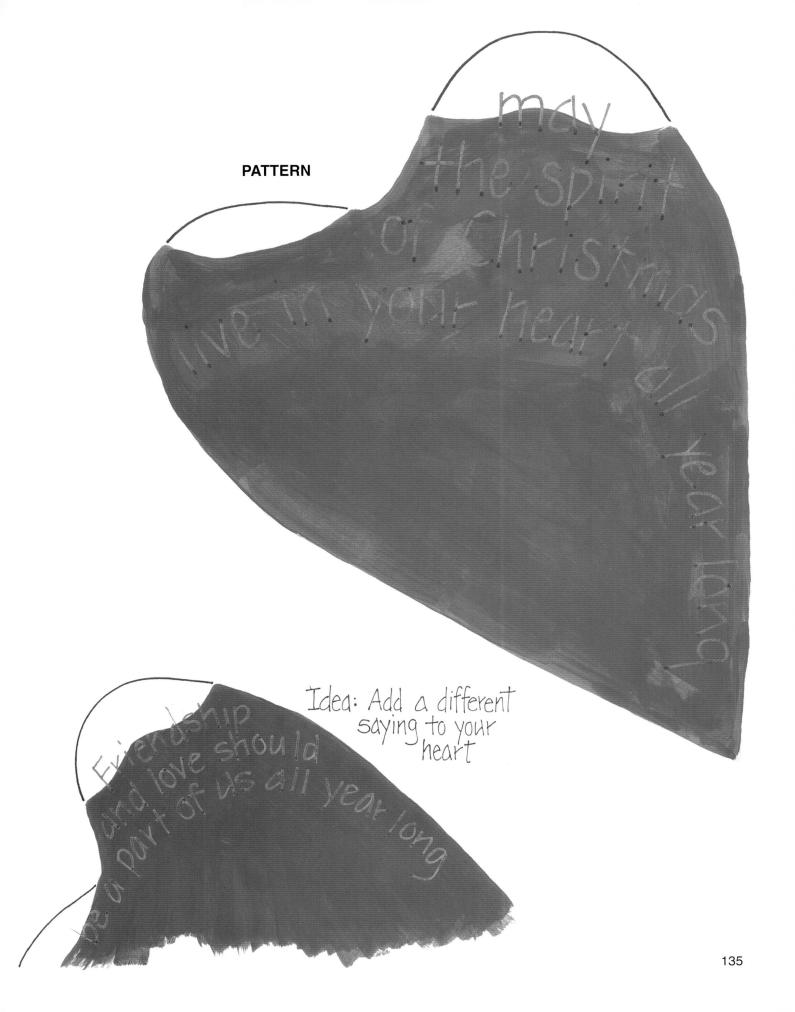

PATTERN

may the spirit of christmas live in your heart all year long

Idea: Add a different saying to your heart

Friendship and love should be a part of us all year long

135

Nine Lives

I saw a little chair that had a moon in the middle of the back. I really liked the idea of an object playing part of the chair back. I loved putting bright colors together on this chair frame to contrast with the simplicity of the black cat.

THINGS YOU'LL NEED:

Chair, 11½" tall with
   ⅝" square legs,
   5¼" wide x
   4¼" deep seat,
   3¾" between back braces
4" x 10" x ½" pine
Wooden bird on a wire,
   1½" high x 3" long
Drill with a ⅛" drill bit
Pencil
Tracing paper
Graphite paper
½" Flat brush
Small pointed brush
Spackling knife
Spackling compound
Medium-grit sandpaper
Fine-grit sandpaper
Clean cloth

Acrylic paint:
   Black
   Buttercrunch
   Melon
   Moon yellow
   Purple
   Turquoise
Fine-point permanent
   black marker
Wood glue
Clear satin spray finish

FOLLOW THESE STEPS:

1 Remove the center of the chair's back. Using a spackling knife, spackle all the holes on the chair with spackling compound. Refer to the General Instructions for spackling and texturing techniques. Let the spackling compound dry completely. Using fine-grit sandpaper, lightly sand the chair. Using a clean, damp cloth, wipe the dust from the chair.

2 Using a ½" flat brush, paint the chair with turquoise acrylic paint. Apply additional coats of acrylic paint until full coverage is achieved. Let the paint dry between coats.

3 Cut the cat's body and the cat's tail from the ½" pine. Use the cat pattern from below. Refer to the General Instructions for transferring patterns. Using medium-grit sandpaper, sand the edges of the cat's body until the cat will fit between the braces on the back of the chair. Using a clean, damp cloth, wipe the dust from the cat's body.

4 Using the ½" flat brush, paint all sides of the cat's body and tail with black acrylic paint. Apply additional coats of acrylic paint until full coverage is achieved. Let the paint dry between coats.

5 Using a pencil, trace the design below onto tracing paper. Using graphite paper, transfer the design onto one side of the cat's body and tail. Using a small pointed brush, paint the design. Refer to the pattern for suggested colors for painting. Apply additional coats of acrylic paint until full coverage is achieved. Let the paint dry between coats.

6 Paint the wooden bird with buttercrunch acrylic paint. Paint the bird's beak with purple acrylic paint. Let

the paint dry between coats. Using the fine-point permanent black marker, dot the eyes on the bird.

7 Slide the cat's body in between the braces on the back of the chair to assure its fit. Once it fits nicely, using wood glue, glue the cat into position. Hold in place until secure. Attach the cat's tail to the chair's seat. Refer to the photograph for suggested placement.

8 Using a drill with a ⅛" drill bit, drill a hole in the top of the chair's brace. Cut the wire on the bottom of the bird to about ¼" long. Using the wood glue, glue the wire into the hole. Hold in place until secure.

9 Using clear satin spray finish, spray the chair. Apply two additional coats of spray finish to the chair. Let the spray finish dry between coats.

PATTERNS

138

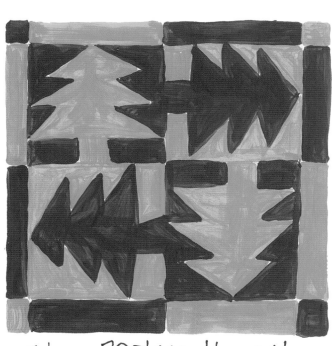

Idea: Replace the cat with a deer & paint the chair seat with a tree motif. Or, how about a house with a path on the chair seat?

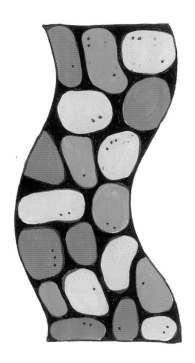

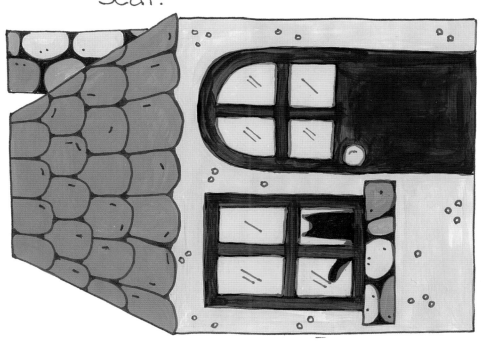

How Now Purple Cow

I am a purple cow. I cannot cook. My husband, Dave, is a marvelous cook. He has a flair with seasonings and can turn an ordinary meal into a treat. He cooks, I clean. In fact, I shop, he cooks, I clean. Maybe I'm not a purple cow, maybe only lavender!

THINGS YOU'LL NEED:

Wooden recipe box,
  $4^{1}/_{4}$" deep x
  $6^{1}/_{2}$" wide x
  $4^{1}/_{2}$" high
Ruler
Pencil
Tracing paper
Graphite paper
$^{1}/_{2}$" Flat brush
Acrylic paint:
  Buttercrunch
  Lavender
  Red
  Turquoise
  White
Fine-point permanent
  black marker
Clear satin spray finish

FOLLOW THESE STEPS:

1 Using a ruler, draw a line $^{1}/_{2}$" from the edge on the lid sides and down the front and back sides of the recipe box with a pencil. Using a $^{1}/_{2}$" flat brush, paint this area with white acrylic paint. Open the lid and paint the inside front rim of the lid with white acrylic paint. Paint the bottom and the sides of the recipe box with red acrylic paint. Paint the back of the recipe box, inside the white colored edge, and the inside of the recipe box with turquoise acrylic paint. Paint the lid of the box inside the white colored edge, and the inside edges of the top, with buttercrunch acrylic paint. Let the paint dry between coats.

2 On the front of the recipe box, measure down 1" from the opening. Draw a horizontal line. Measure up 1" from the bottom of the recipe box. Draw a horizontal line. Paint the center with buttercrunch acrylic paint. Paint the top and the bottom with turquoise acrylic paint. Let the paint dry between coats. Refer to the photograph.

3 Using the pencil, trace the lettering design and the floral pattern from page 142 onto tracing paper. Using graphite paper, transfer the

lettering design onto the front of the recipe box. Trace the cow pattern below onto tracing paper. Using graphite paper, transfer the design onto the lid of the recipe box.

4 Using the 1/2" flat brush, paint the cow with lavender acrylic paint. Paint the cow's spots with white acrylic paint. Using a small pointed brush, paint some of the flowers with lavender acrylic paint and some with red acrylic paint. Paint the leaves with turquoise acrylic paint. Let the paint dry between coats. Refer to the pattern for suggested colors for painting.

5 Using a fine-point permanent black marker, outline the letters and the flowers. Add the curly lines in the center of each flower. Add small dots. Refer to the pattern for suggested placement. Outline the cow and draw the eyes and nostrils. Add dots around the cow's body. Refer to the pattern for suggested placement. Let the marker dry.

6 Using the pencil, draw three vertical lines in the white painted area on the sides of the recipe box. Draw perpendicular lines through the vertical lines to create squares. Lift the lid. Draw the same squares along the inside front rim. Draw the same squares inside the white spots on the cow. Using the fine-point permanent black marker, color alternating squares. Don't worry if some of the white

acrylic paint shows through. Let the marker dry.

7 Using clear satin spray finish, spray the outside of the recipe box. Let the spray finish dry. Spray the inside of the recipe box. Keep the lid open so it will not stick. Let the spray finish dry. Apply a second coat of spray finish to the recipe box. Let the spray finish dry between coats.

PATTERNS

Metric Conversions

INCHES TO MILLIMETRES AND CENTIMETRES
MM-Millimetres   CM-Centimetres

INCHES	MM	CM	INCHES	CM	INCHES	CM
$1/8$	3	0.9	9	22.9	30	76.2
$1/4$	6	0.6	10	25.4	31	78.7
$3/8$	10	1.0	11	27.9	32	81.3
$1/2$	13	1.3	12	30.5	33	83.8
$5/8$	16	1.6	13	33.0	34	86.4
$3/4$	19	1.9	14	35.6	35	88.9
$7/8$	22	2.2	15	38.1	36	91.4
1	25	2.5	16	40.6	37	94.0
$1 1/4$	32	3.2	17	43.2	38	96.5
$1 1/2$	38	3.8	18	45.7	39	99.1
$1 3/4$	44	4.4	19	48.3	40	101.6
2	51	5.1	20	50.8	41	104.1
$2 1/2$	64	6.4	21	53.3	42	106.7
3	76	7.6	22	55.9	43	109.2
$3 1/2$	89	8.9	23	58.4	44	111.8
4	102	10.2	24	61.0	45	114.3
$4 1/2$	114	11.4	25	63.5	46	116.8
5	127	12.7	26	66.0	47	119.4
6	152	15.2	27	68.6	48	121.9
7	178	17.8	28	71.1	49	124.5
8	203	20.3	29	73.7	50	127.0

YARDS TO METRES

YARDS	METRES	YARDS	METRES	YARDS	METRES	YARDS	METRES	YARDS	METRES
$1/8$	0.11	$2 1/8$	1.94	$4 1/8$	3.77	$6 1/8$	5.60	$8 1/8$	7.43
$1/4$	0.23	$2 1/4$	2.06	$4 1/4$	3.89	$6 1/4$	5.72	$8 1/4$	7.54
$3/8$	0.34	$2 3/8$	2.17	$4 3/8$	4.00	$6 3/8$	5.83	$8 3/8$	7.66
$1/2$	0.46	$2 1/2$	2.29	$4 1/2$	4.11	$6 1/2$	5.94	$8 1/2$	7.77
$5/8$	0.57	$2 5/8$	2.40	$4 5/8$	4.23	$6 5/8$	6.06	$8 5/8$	7.89
$3/4$	0.69	$2 3/4$	2.51	$4 3/4$	4.34	$6 3/4$	6.17	$8 3/4$	8.00
$7/8$	0.80	$2 7/8$	2.63	$4 7/8$	4.46	$6 7/8$	6.29	$8 7/8$	8.12
1	0.91	3	2.74	5	4.57	7	6.40	9	8.23
$1 1/8$	1.03	$3 1/8$	2.86	$5 1/8$	4.69	$7 1/8$	6.52	$9 1/8$	8.34
$1 1/4$	1.14	$3 1/4$	2.97	$5 1/4$	4.80	$7 1/4$	6.63	$9 1/4$	8.46
$1 3/8$	1.26	$3 3/8$	3.09	$5 3/8$	4.91	$7 3/8$	6.74	$9 3/8$	8.57
$1 1/2$	1.37	$3 1/2$	3.20	$5 1/2$	5.03	$7 1/2$	6.86	$9 1/2$	8.69
$1 5/8$	1.49	$3 5/8$	3.31	$5 5/8$	5.14	$7 5/8$	6.97	$9 5/8$	8.80
$1 3/4$	1.60	$3 3/4$	3.43	$5 3/4$	5.26	$7 3/4$	7.09	$9 3/4$	8.92
$1 7/8$	1.71	$3 7/8$	3.54	$5 7/8$	5.37	$7 7/8$	7.20	$9 7/8$	9.03
2	1.83	4	3.66	6	5.49	8	7.32	10	9.14

Index